P9-CLR-775

Geography of the United States

Teaching the Five Themes

by Ted Henson

illustrated by Tom Heggie

cover design by Jeff Van Kanegan
Photo credit: GlobeShots™

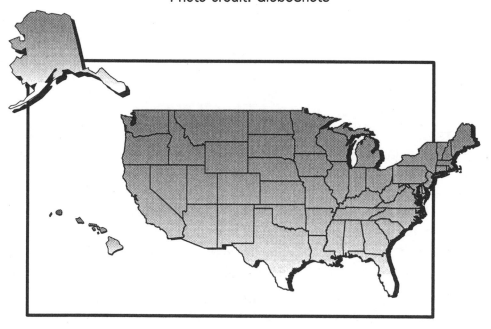

Publisher
Instructional Fair • TS Denison
Grand Rapids, Michigan 49544

Instructional Fair • TS Denison grants the individual purchaser permission to reproduce patterns and student activity materials in this book for noncommercial individual or classroom use only. Reproduction for an entire school or school system is strictly prohibited. No other part of this publication may be reproduced in whole or in part. No part of this publication may be reproduced for storage in a retrieval system, or transmitted in any form or by any means, electronic, mechanical, recording, or otherwise, without the prior written permission of the publisher. For information regarding permission write to Instructional Fair • TS Denison, P.O. Box 1650, Grand Rapids, MI 49501.

ISBN: 1-56822-436-2
Geography of the United States
© GlobeShots™
Copyright © 1997 by Instructional Fair • TS Denison
2400 Turner Avenue NW
Grand Rapids, Michigan 49544

All Right Reserved • Printed in the USA

Table of Contents

Introduction

This book presents an overview of the geography of the United States. The method used involves an application of the five themes of geography to the study of the United States. The use of the five themes allows the teacher to go beyond just the physical geography and to include cultural characteristics of the United States as well. The first unit of study provides a brief review of the five themes of geography and what is included in each theme.

The book is designed to allow the teacher to teach each of the units in its entirety or select the information and activities that will supplement those already planned for the classroom. Each unit provides student activity sheets containing information for the students to read to expand their knowledge. Questions are then given to ensure the understanding of the information. Next, activities are suggested. There are two types of activities. Some activities are self-contained in the book, ready for students to complete. Others are suggested activities that will require research and additional materials for completion. These activities may be done in either small groups or by individual students. The activities are written to allow teachers to make changes or adapt them to their students' needs.

Each unit of study also provides the teacher with goals, objectives, rationales, and vocabulary lists. The goals and objectives may be used as they are stated, or the teacher may design his or her own. The rationale for the unit is designed to provide the teacher with the answer to the eternal question, "Why do I have to do this?" The vocabulary words are listed on the unit introduction pages and are indicated in italics on the student activity pages. In most cases, definitions are provided on the student activity pages.

Background information is given for each unit as the activities are introduced on the teacher pages. The information is designed to help the teacher gain a feeling for what is to be accomplished with each task and to provide any additional information that might be needed. A recommended lesson plan is also included for each student activity sheet. The lesson plans are simply a guide to serve as a springboard for the teacher's own creativity.

The aim of this book is to provide a study of the geography of the United States while making practical use of the five themes of geography. Every effort has been made to make the study both interesting and challenging. If students completing this study find that they have a clearer understanding of the geography of the United States and of the five themes of geography, then the goals for the book have been realized.

The Five Themes of Geography

Goals for This Unit

Students will
1. explain the meaning of each of the five themes of geography.
2. complete activities illustrating each of the themes.
3. use atlases and reference books to gather and classify information.
4. use the five themes to explain the geography of their home areas.

Rationale

The study of the geography of the United States is a very broad topic. It is important to have a framework in which to carry out the study. The five themes of geography provide such a framework. The themes give a broad definition to the term *geography*, not only by looking at physical characteristics of the nation, but also by examining the cultural characteristics that make the United States what it is today. This broad approach is important in gaining a clear picture of the entire nation. Each of the themes will be used as the regions of the United States are examined in this book. Therefore, it is important to have a good understanding of the five themes of geography.

Skills Taught in This Unit

brainstorming	using reference books, atlases
descriptive writing	mapping skills
classifying information	analyzing information

Vocabulary

absolute location	*parallels*
equator	*meridians of longitude*
latitude	*relative location*
prime meridian	*hemispheres*
place geography	*physical characteristics*
human characteristics	*human-environment interaction*
consequence	*movement*
interdependent	*region*

Background Information

In studying the geography of any area of the world, the five themes of geography provide a basic outline that allows students to expand their study beyond mere maps and site location. The word *geography* means the study of the earth. However, too often a narrow view is taken about what makes up the study. In a study of the United States, emphasis should be placed on the physical and cultural makeup of the regions. The five themes allow this to happen and provide a framework in which to fashion the study. This introductory unit will review for students the five themes of geography which will be used in the study of the United States.

The Theme of Location

The first theme of geography seeks to answer the primary question, "Where is it located?" This theme introduces the two types of location—*absolute* and *relative*. Absolute location provides an exact spot on the face of the earth. A street address is an example of absolute location. A street address helps pinpoint the exact location of a house or business. Latitude and longitude are also used to help find exact locations on the face of the earth. Imaginary grid lines are drawn on the map or globe and location is defined in degrees of latitude (north or south of the equator) or degrees of longitude (east or west of the prime meridian).

Relative location is not as exact as absolute location. Relative location helps to locate one site by telling its position in relation to other sites. For example, North Carolina is located north of Georgia and South Carolina, east of Tennessee, south of Virginia and west of the Atlantic Ocean. By giving these relationships, a clearer picture is formed about the location of the state of North Carolina. This lesson will demonstrate both types of location.

Objectives
Students will
1. use an atlas to solve problems of location.
2. use relative location clues to identify states and other physical features in the United States.

Materials: pencils, classroom set of atlases, "The Theme of Location" activity sheets

Procedure
1. Review with students the theme of location. Ask the class to read the material explaining the theme provided in "The Theme of Location" activity sheets.
2. Discuss the theme of location in class. Ask students to give examples of how both absolute and relative location can provide helpful information.
3. Students should use atlases to solve the problems in absolute location. Make certain the correct symbols are used in writing the latitude and longitude notations.
4. Atlases or maps of the United States will assist students in solving the relative location activity. As students finish this activity, ask them to write some additional problems for their fellow students to solve.

The Theme of Place

The second theme of geography is *place*. Place geography deals with describing the physical and human characteristics of a site. Physical characteristics include a description of the site as nature provided it. These descriptions include the land, soil, water sources, topography, and other features of nature that are present. Human characteristics complete the picture by describing the people who live at the site. This description takes into account ethnic groups, religious affiliations, socioeconomic levels, educational levels, recreational pastimes, and other descriptions of the people. This lesson will introduce students to some of the characteristics considered in the theme of place.

Objectives
Students will
1. define *place geography* and the two types of characteristics involved.
2. write descriptive paragraphs of their home area, giving both human and physical characteristics.
3. use descriptions of human and physical characteristics to identify specific locations.

Materials: paper, pencils, "The Theme of Place" activity sheet

Procedure
1. Assign the reading of "The Theme of Place" activity sheet. Lead a discussion of the meaning of human and physical characteristics.
2. Students should answer the three questions for review and then discuss their answers in a small group.
3. Before students begin writing the paper describing their home area, brainstorm a list of human and physical characteristics that might be used in the description. After the papers are completed and read to the class, add additional characteristics that were given in any of the descriptions.
4. The descriptions written by students of their favorite places in the United States may be used in a game. Divide the class into two groups. Each student reads his or her description to the opposing team. If that team gives a correct answer, it scores one point. If not, no points are awarded. The team with the most points wins the game.
5. After the game, review some of the human and physical characteristics that were described in the paragraphs so students have a complete knowledge of the theme of place.

The Theme of Human-Environment Interaction

The third theme of geography is *human-environment interaction*. This theme closely relates to many topics covered in science. Human-environment interaction looks at changes people have made in the natural environment of a particular area. One characteristic of humankind is the need to make changes so that life will be easier. For that purpose, houses were constructed for protection from the elements, roads were built to make travel easier, and factories were built to increase the production of goods that were needed. This constant change is evident in our daily lives. This lesson will look at examples of changes people have made in their environment and the need to consider the consequences before changes are made.

Objectives

Students will

1. define the theme of *human-environment interaction*.
2. explain why considering the consequences of changes in the environment is of vital importance.
3. compile a list of changes in the local environment that have occurred within the last 50 years.

Materials: paper, pencils, chart paper, markers, "The Theme of Human-Environment Interaction" activity sheet

Procedure

1. Assign the reading of "The Theme of Human-Environment Interaction" activity sheet. Discuss with the class examples of ways people have changed the environment over the years. Ask students to consider any consequences that had to be considered when changes were made in the environment.
2. In a class discussion, look at the questions given for review. Students may answer the questions on paper before the discussion begins. The important issues to consider are that people constantly change their environment and that often consequences result from these changes. The issue must be whether the advantages of making the change outweigh the consequences that must be faced. Consideration must also be given to whether the change on the environment will be positive or negative.
3. Provide each small group with markers and a sheet of chart paper to use in compiling its list of changes that have occurred over the last 50 years in the local area. Each group should then share its list with the class. For each change listed, the group should evaluate the change as being positive or negative and give supporting reasons.

The Theme of Movement

Movement of people, goods, and ideas is the fourth theme of geography. This theme looks at all types of movement and the effects they have on the people and the environment. The movement of people has been fundamental to the settlement of the United States. People came to this country for a variety of reasons. In fact, the United States is often called "a nation of immigrants." As people move, they carry with them cultural baggage that affects the way they live in their new home. The weight of this cultural baggage should be considered before moves are made.

The movement of ideas and products has an effect on each of us every day of our lives. With the use of satellites, events halfway around the world are brought into our living rooms as they happen. We are no longer isolated from the impact of wars, famines, or diseases. At the same time, each time we sit down to eat, there is a very good chance that we are eating products from around the world. Global interdependence is becoming a reality that we must all accept and understand if we are to be responsible global citizens. This lesson will examine the importance of movement in all aspects of our lives.

Objectives

Students will

1. identify the three areas of movement covered by this theme of geography.
2. explain how movement affects each of us in our daily lives.
3. explore global interdependence by identifying products and countries of origin.

Materials: paper, pencils, chart paper, markers, "The Theme of Movement" activity sheet

Procedure

1. Ask students to identify examples of movement that they observe each day. List these examples on the board.
2. Assign the reading of "The Theme of Movement" activity sheet. After the reading has been completed, ask students to add to their list of movements.
3. Students should answer the three review questions, then participate in a class discussion of movement and its impact on our daily lives.
4. The activity will allow students to see how interdependent the world is becoming by looking at the origin of objects that touch their lives each day. Compile the class list on chart paper.
5. As a follow-up, ask students to choose five items from the list of products and trace on a world map the route the products might have taken to reach their classroom. Students should include the modes of transportation that might have been used.

The Theme of Region

The fifth theme of geography is *region*. Region was a tool designed by humans to help them better understand the world in which they live. The idea was that by dividing the world into regions, it would be easier to gain an understanding of this complex world. A region is an area that has at least one common characteristic that separates it from surrounding areas. Regions may be based on political divisions, physical features, cultural characteristics, or many other types of characteristics. In this lesson, students will examine the concept of regions and identify some of the types of regions in the United States.

Objectives

Students will

1. explain the meaning of *region* and give examples of regions within their state.
2. identify some of the types of regions found in the United States.

Materials: paper, pencil, "The Theme of Region" activity sheet

Procedure

1. Ask students to read "The Theme of Region" activity sheet. Students should answer and then discuss in class the three review questions.

2. Brainstorm a list of regions, identify their types (political, agricultural, etc.), and write them on the board.
3. Ask students to identify regions within their state and tell the type of region they represent. Discuss this list in class.
4. Students should complete the second activity by telling the type of region that is represented in each listing. After this is completed, ask students to make up their own list for another student to solve.

Conclusion

The five themes of geography are useful tools in the study of the United States. The activities in this book will attempt to use these tools to provide a picture of both the physical and cultural features of the nation. Students need to have a working knowledge of the themes so that they will gain a better understanding of the factors that have made the United States the country it is today.

The Theme of Location

The first fundamental question asked in geography is, "Where is it located?" In attempting to answer that question, geographers use the theme of *location*. Location can be defined in two ways—*absolute* and *relative*. Both of these methods provide useful information when attempting to answer the question, "Where is it located?"

Absolute location deals with an exact location on the face of the earth. One example of absolute location is a street address. However, on a map or globe, the use of a street address is not always practical. For this reason, maps use imaginary grid lines to help find the correct location of a site. The lines that run east and west are called *parallels*. These parallels measure *latitude*, the distance north or south of the equator. The *equator* is an imaginary line that runs around the center of the earth.

Parallels of latitude are measured in degrees. Latitude measures start from the equator which is 0°. The parallels run as far north as the north pole, which is 90° North. They run as far south as the South Pole, which is 90° South. Thus, the equator divides the earth into two equal hemispheres, the Northern Hemisphere and the Southern Hemisphere.

Each place on the face of the earth is located at a line of latitude either north or south of the equator. Degrees of latitude may be broken down further into minutes and seconds. A site that is located at 35°, 15 minutes, and 20 seconds north latitude would be written as 35° 15' 20" N. The direction from the equator, either north or south, must be given after any notation.

The earth also has imaginary lines that run north and south on a map or globe. These lines are called *meridians of longitude*. They measure the distance east or west of the *prime meridian*. The prime meridian (0°) is a line running through Greenwich Observatory just outside of London, England. The prime meridian also divides the world into two equal *hemispheres*, the Eastern Hemisphere and the Western Hemisphere.

Lines of longitude run east or west of the prime meridian to the International Date Line, which is 180°. Thus, the two hemispheres measure a complete circle of 360°. A site located at 100°, 40 minutes, and 15 seconds east of the prime meridian would be written as 100° 40' 15" E. By using the grid system of latitude and longitude, it is possible to determine the exact location of any site on the earth.

A second type of location is *relative location*. Often relative location is more helpful than knowing the latitude or longitude of a place. Relative location tells where a site is located in relationship to other places. For example, Utah is located south of Idaho and Wyoming, west of Colorado, east of Nevada, and north of Arizona. If a person is familiar with the Rocky Mountain States, the relative location given for Utah would help create a clear picture of its location.

Student Activities

Complete each of the following problems using absolute location.

1. The following major cities are identified by their latitude and longitude positions. Use an atlas to identify the cities. Give both the city and state.
   a. 38° 52' N, 77° W _____
   b. 47° 41' N, 122° 15' W _____
   c. 38° 40' N, 90° 12' W _____
   d. 32° 50' N, 96° 50' W _____
   e. 41° 53' N, 87° 40' W _____

2. For each of the following cities, give its latitude and longitude.
   a. Phoenix, Arizona _____
   b. San Francisco, California _____
   c. Charlotte, North Carolina _____
   d. Indianapolis, Indiana _____
   e. Denver, Colorado _____

Complete the following activity using relative location. Use the clues to name each state.

3. This state is surrounded by Minnesota, Wisconsin, Illinois, Missouri, Nebraska, and South Dakota. The state is _____.

4. This state has Lake Erie and Michigan to the north, Indiana to the west, Kentucky and West Virginia to the south, and Pennsylvania to the east.
   The state is _____.

5. This state has Texas to the west, Arkansas to the north, Mississippi to the east, and the Gulf of Mexico to the south. The state is_____.

6. This river empties into the Gulf of California after flowing through California, Nevada, Arizona, Utah, and Colorado. The river is the _____.

7. These hills are located in southwestern South Dakota and northeastern Wyoming. They are just west of Rapid City, South Dakota. They are called _____.

The Theme of Place

Place is the second theme of geography. *Place geography* attempts to describe the site. This is done by giving both human and physical characteristics. The two types of characteristics help to provide a clear description of any site.

Physical characteristics deal with the natural setting of the area. For example, the land may be flat, hilly, or mountainous. The soil could be sandy or clay. The land might be a forest, or it might be a prairie. A river might run nearby or the site could be located near an ocean. All of these are examples of physical characteristics.

Human characteristics include the people who live in an area. What do they do for a living? What ethnic groups are represented? What is the educational level of the people? What are the major religions in the area? What are the major types of recreation? What is the average age level of the people? Answers to these questions and other similar ones help to provide a description of the people who live at a site.

Student Activities

Answer the following questions based on the selection above.

1. What is *place geography*? _____

2. What two types of characteristics are considered in place geography? _____

_____

3. Why are both types of characteristics important in getting a clear picture of a particular site? _____

4. Write a paper describing your home area. Include in the paper details about the physical features found in the area and characteristics of the people who live there. Compare your descriptions to others in your class. Compile a list of physical and human characteristics of your home area.

5. Think of a place that you would most like to visit in the United States. Write a one-paragraph description of the place. Describe both physical and human characteristics. Be certain not to mention the name of the place in your paragraph. Read your paragraph to other students and let them try to guess your favorite spot.

The Theme of Human-Environment Interaction

The third theme of geography is *human-environment interaction*. This theme looks at how people have changed their environments. Change is one thing that is always present. From the very beginning, people have attempted to make changes so life could be more enjoyable. This process of change is the concept of human-environment interaction.

When the early settlers came to the New World, they began to clear land so that houses could be built. Trees were cut and construction began. The clearing of land, cutting of trees, and building of houses are all examples of human-environment interaction.

In modern times, roads are built to provide an efficient interstate system across the nation. Dams are built to provide water for irrigation and human consumption. Malls are built to regulate the temperature and provide attractive shopping areas. Efforts to change the environment are constantly occurring and will probably continue indefinitely.

When changes are made in the environment, there is usually a *consequence* that has to be considered. For example, if a dam is built on a river to control the floods that have been occurring, how much land will be flooded as a result of the lake that forms behind the dam? If a field is paved to make way for a parking garage, where will the water run when it rains? Consideration should always be given to whether the change is worth the consequences that go with it. Failure to consider the consequences of change can be disastrous.

Student Activities

Answer the following questions.

1. What is meant by *human-environment interaction*? _____

   _____

2. Why is it critical to consider consequences when making changes in our environment? _____

3. What are some examples of human-environment interaction currently occurring in your area? What were the consequences that had to be considered when making the changes? Write the list on the back of this sheet.

Work in small groups to research changes that have occurred in your home area within the last 50 years. Check reference books, old newspapers, and magazines and interview your parents. Compile a list to share with the class.

Name _____

The Theme of Movement

Movement is the fourth theme of geography. In the study of movement, consideration is given to the movement of people, goods, and ideas. People move for a variety of reasons, and each move brings about change. Goods move daily and help to keep the economy flowing. Ideas are carried across the waves on radios, televisions, telephones, and computers. We live in a world full of movement.

The movement of people takes into account why they moved and where they went. From the first settlers on the east coast to the pioneers traveling west in covered wagons, movement has been important in the development of the United States. Whether the motivation for movement was freedom or gold, each person helped to make the nation what it is today.

The movement of goods and ideas has global impact. The world is becoming more and more *interdependent*. Goods are shipped around the world for consumption. Economies are dependent upon the selling of goods in other countries. Modern technology brings events happening around the world into our living rooms as they occur. This theme of geography demonstrates the importance of being globally literate, so that good decisions can be made in business and in government.

Student Activities

Answer each of the following questions.

1. The theme of movement considers the movement of the following: _____, _____, and_____.

2. Why does the movement of people, goods, and ideas have a global effect on each of us? _____

3. What types of changes occur when people move?_____

We are in touch with products from around the world every day without realizing it. Work in a group with two or three other students and check items you have at your desk or in your pocket to see where they were made. Do not forget to check labels in clothing and shoes. Make a list of each product and the state or country in which it was produced. Share your list with other groups and make a compiled list for the class.

The Theme of Region

The fifth theme of geography is *region*. Regions are designated by humans in an effort to gain a better understanding of the world in which we live. A region is an area with at least one common characteristic that makes it different from the surrounding areas. The key is that there must be at least one identifying characteristic for a region to exist.

There are many types of regions. The United States is a political region made up of 50 smaller regions called states. The Appalachian Highlands is a physical region made up of the various mountain ranges in the Appalachian region. The Corn Belt is an agricultural region in the Midwestern states that produces large quantities of corn. Regions may be created around a wide variety of characteristics.

Student Activities

Answer the following questions.

1. What is a region? _____

2. Why are regions usually created? _____

3. Name some of the types of regions. _____

4. What regions are identified within your home state? Make a list of the regions and tell what type of region they represent (political, physical, cultural, etc.).

   _____

   _____

   _____

5. Identify the type of region named in each of the following:

   Montana _____   Rocky Mountains _____

   Cotton Belt _____   Little Havana _____

   Great Lakes _____   District of Columbia _____

   Chicago _____   Chinatown _____

New England

Goals for This Unit

Students will
1. use atlases to find the absolute and relative locations of sites in New England.
2. demonstrate the concept of plate tectonics and the effect it has had on New England.
3. identify physical features that make up the ten physical regions of New England.
4. illustrate how people have used the physical features of New England to shape their lives.
5. research various inventors from New England and explain their contributions to American society.
6. apply all five themes of geography to the study of New England.

Rationale

New England is a small section of the United States, located in the extreme northeastern corner of the nation. It has played a vital role in the development of the nation. It was in New England that the first major battles of the American Revolution were fought, around the colonial seaport of Boston. Many historic sites and events are commemorated in the area. Later, New England became the first industrialized region of the country. The swiftly flowing streams helped to produce the power to operate factories that were built beside them. Industry continues to play a vital role in the lives of the people there. The study of New England provides a view of one of the earliest settled regions of the nation. This region is noted for its scenic beauty and the proud independent traditions of its people.

Skills Taught in This Unit

developing time lines
reading and interpreting charts
calculating percentages
interpreting themes of geography
illustrating concepts

using atlases and reference books
writing creatively
working with maps
constructing models

Vocabulary

moraines
reforestation
drumlins
plate tectonics

textiles
mountains
lowlands
multicultural

Industrial Revolution
interchangeable parts
integrated textile factory

Background Information

The growth and development of New England is illustrated in this unit. Students will directly apply the five themes of geography to their study of this region. As the study progresses, ask students to keep in mind the themes that are being used in each activity. These themes will help to provide a framework on which to base the study of New England.

Location in New England

Themes of Geography: Location

This activity will engage students in identifying the absolute and relative locations of various states in New England. They will need to be aware of the meaning of absolute and relative location before completing the activity.

Objectives
Students will
1. use an atlas to determine which state is being identified by specific degrees of latitude and longitude.
2. use relative location clues to identify the New England states.
3. read maps in an atlas to answer questions about New England.

Materials: classroom atlases, pencils, "Location in New England" activity sheets

Procedure
1. Review with students the two types of location—absolute and relative.
2. Provide copies of the "Location in New England" activity sheets for each student. Students may work independently or in small groups to complete the activity.

The Forming of New England

Themes of Geography: Location, Place, Movement, Region

The concept of plate tectonics is introduced to students in this activity. The printed material briefly explains the constant moving of plates across the surface of the earth and the interaction of these plates. New England is used as an example of how these interactions have affected the earth. Several collisions of the crustal plates caused New England to have the physical form that it has today. Examples of these forms are discussed in this lesson.

Objectives
Students will
1. answer questions based on the written text.
2. construct models to demonstrate the movement of continental plates during the history of the world.
3. construct a model to show how mountains can be lifted up by the collision of plates.

Materials: *National Geographic Atlas of the World* and other reference books, multiple copies of world outline maps, scissors, glue (paste), blue construction paper, clay, pencils, felt pins, "The Forming of New England" activity sheets

Procedure
1. Review with students the concept of plate tectonics. Use reference books such as the *National Geographic Atlas of the World* to help with the explanation and to provide illustrations. Ask students to read the material provided with "The Forming of New England" activity sheets.
2. Review the material by assigning the questions on the activity sheet. Students may work independently or with a partner to find answers. Go over the questions in class.
3. Activity number 7 at the bottom of the activity sheet asks students to research and prepare reports on plate tectonics. Make certain that sufficient reference books are available for this activity. Reports may be compiled by individuals or small groups.
4. The research completed in making the reports on plate tectonics should help students in completing the remaining activities. Expect to see variations on how Pangaea was formed. The important thing is gaining a knowledge of the concept of plate tectonics.

Life in New England

Themes of Geography: Location, Place, Human-Environment Interaction Movement, Region

The people of New England have a reputation of being proud and independent. From the early settlements, they have taken what nature provided and worked with it to make a living. Farming, while not as widespread as it once was, is still practiced in areas across the region. New England became the first industrialized area of the nation, and industry continues to be an important part of the region. In addition, occupations in fishing, shipping, and forest products continue to be found in various parts of the area.

As their occupations have changed, so have the people in New England. There have been large influxes of Irish, Italians, and French Canadians, along with Germans, Portuguese, African Americans, East Europeans, and others. The cities of New England have taken on a multicultural atmosphere. This lesson will explore some of the changes that have occurred in the life of New England.

Objectives
Students will
1. answer questions as a review of the material read.
2. explain the process of reforestation and use New England as an example of a successful reforestation project.
3. make a drawing or model to demonstrate the use of water power to operate a business.

Materials: chart paper, pencils, reference materials, drawing paper, colored pencils, crayons, art supplies, "Life in New England" activity sheets

Procedure

1. Ask students to read the material provided in the activity sheets. As they read, they should make notes of some of the changes that have occurred in New England over the years. Lead a discussion of these changes. Compile a list on the board or on chart paper.
2. After the discussion, the four review questions should be answered and discussed.
3. Students will need to research the process known as *reforestation*. After gaining an understanding of the process, ask students to research what has happened in New England and how that has proven successful.
4. The final activity will require researching the use of water power in early factories. Students may either draw a series of pictures explaining how the process worked, or they might build a model. The important point is that water was used to turn a wheel, which in turn caused other wheels and levers to operate.

Inventors of New England

Themes of Geography: Place, Movement, Human-Environment Interaction

The United States entered the Industrial Revolution on the strength of men and women who had dreams and followed them through to completion. Many inventions played major roles in making the United States an industrialized nation. New England was home to many of these inventors. This lesson will introduce students to some of the inventors who called New England home and give practice in using information in charts and completing that information.

Objectives

Students will
1. research and complete the information given about selected inventors in a chart.
2. construct a time line showing major historic events and the inventors being studied.
3. write a monologue, role-playing one of the inventors mentioned.

Materials: pencils, reference books, construction paper, yarn, note cards, magic markers, "Inventors of New England" activity sheets

Procedure

1. Discuss with students the role that inventors have played in the history of the United States. Following the discussion, read the material provided on the activity sheets.
2. Students should use reference books to complete the chart on inventors.
3. Students may construct one time line for the class or individual time lines. Directions for a classroom time line are given in activity 2 on the activity sheets. Individual time lines may be done by drawing a line across a sheet of drawing paper. Lines of different color may be used to divide the base line into the decades. The necessary information may be added by printing with colored markers directly onto the paper.
4. When students have completed the research on their chosen inventors and written their monologues, stage a television show in the class in which the inventors come back to talk about their achievements. Students should dress in costumes of the appropriate period to tell about their inventors.

The New England States

New England is a small region of the United States composed of six political regions. These political regions are Maine, Vermont, New Hampshire, Massachusetts, Rhode Island, and Connecticut. In this lesson, students will use information given in a chart to answer questions and solve problems. Mathematics computation skills will also be used in this lesson.

Objectives

Students will
1. answer questions using information given in a chart.
2. research to find additional information needed but not shown on the chart.
3. color a map of New England identifying states and capitals.

Materials: colored pencils, pencil, calculator (optional), reference books, "The New England States" activity sheets

Procedure

1. Students should understand that a state is a form of a political region. Ask students to identify the six political regions that make up New England.
2. Students should use the information in the chart to answer questions 1-4. A calculator may be used to calculate the percentages if desired.
3. Question 5 will require the use of reference books. Allow students time to do research to answer the question correctly.
4. Students should use colored pencils to complete the map and label the states and capitals.

Conclusion

New England is a region with a long, proud history. It is an example of a region that has experienced continuous change. These changes have also brought about challenges. The people of New England continue to work to meet these challenges. Geography has played a large role in the development of this area and will continue to do so in the future. Successful projects such as the reforestation of the region help to show that people can protect the natural resources that are so vital to everyone.

Location in New England

New England, which consists of Maine, New Hampshire, Vermont, Massachusetts, Connecticut, and Rhode Island, is the most northeastern region of the United States. The land is bounded by Long Island on the south, the Atlantic Ocean on the east, the Saint Lawrence River and Canada on the north, and New York on the west. The Connecticut River is the longest river. The Green and White Mountain Ranges, a part of the Appalachian Highlands, form the major highlands of the region.

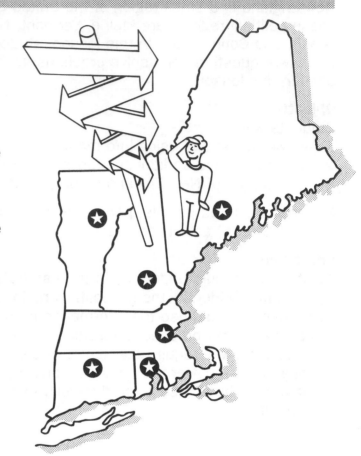

The coastline of New England includes capes and inlets, twisting 6,130 miles (9,865 kilometers) from southern Connecticut to northern Maine. The land features fractured rock with thin layers of soil which rises to the peaks of the Appalachians. The region is sparsely populated in the north, but cities dot the southern areas.

Student Activities

1. Each of the six states in New England has an absolute location using degrees of latitude and longitude. Use an atlas to find which state you would be in if you were at the following points:

   Degrees of Latitude/Longitude   State

   a. Latitude   44° N
      Longitude   73° W   _____

   b. Latitude   45° N
      Longitude   69° W   _____

   c. Latitude   41° 45' N
      Longitude   71° 30' W   _____

   d. Latitude   43° N
      Longitude   72° W   _____

e. Latitude 42° 20' N
   Longitude 72° W
   _____

f. Latitude 41° 45' N
   Longitude 73° W
   _____

2. Use the relative location clues given below to identify each of the New England States.

   a. This state is bordered on the east by Maine and the Atlantic Ocean, the north by Quebec, the west by Vermont, and the south by Massachusetts.
      _____

   b. This state is bordered by Massachusetts on the north, Rhode Island on the east, New York on the west, and the Atlantic Ocean on the south.
      _____

   c. This state is bordered by New Brunswick on the east, the Atlantic Ocean on the south, Quebec on the north, and New Hampshire on the west.
      _____

   d. This smallest state is bordered by Massachusetts on the east and north, the Atlantic Ocean on the south, and Connecticut on the west.
      _____

   e. This New England state is bordered by five other states including New York.
      _____

   f. This state is bordered by Quebec on the north, New York on the west, New Hampshire on the east, and Massachusetts on the south.
      _____

3. Use the atlas to complete the following statements about the New England region.

   a. The river forming the border between Vermont and New Hampshire and running through both Massachusetts and Connecticut is called the _____ River.

   b. The large lake which forms part of the border between New York and Vermont and extends into Canada is called _____.

   c. The Massachusetts cape which looks like a crooked finger is called _____ _____.

   d. The New England state which extends the farthest north is _____.

   e. The New England state which extends the farthest south is _____.

   f. Narragansett Bay is located on the southeastern edge of the state of _____ _____.

   g. The Penobscot River flows through the state of _____ into the Penobscot Bay.

   h. The major mountain range crossing the New England States is the _____ _____.

The Forming of New England

The earth's crust and the top portion of the mantle form a rigid shell around the earth that is broken into huge sections called *plates*. The heat from the center of the earth causes slow, constant movement of these plates. The movement and interaction of these plates is called *plate tectonics* and contributes to the building of continents.

The region known as New England is a creation of plate tectonic collisions and glacial grinding. The first impact of crustal plates in the New England region occurred some 250 million years ago. At that time the African, European, and North American plates collided. The result was that some slabs of the earth's crust were hurled hundreds of miles westward. This collision meant that portions of the current Appalachian Mountains might have risen as high as the Himalayas are today. However, the process of erosion began immediately.

About 180 million years ago, a super continent was formed when all the continental plates collided. The super continent was called *Pangaea*. Pangaea was surrounded by one large ocean known as *Panthalassa*. This collision caused heavy erosion to the Appalachians. As erosion occurred, sediment formed much of New York and Pennsylvania and spread as far west as Ohio. As the weight of the sediment diminished, the earth's surface below began to rise. Thus, the scenic *mountains* of New England today are merely uplifted roots of those once colossal ranges.

Several million years later, another crustal plate collision occurred, triggering volcanoes and granite intrusions. Two results of this collision are Maine's Mount Katahdin and Vermont's famous Barre granite. Finally, about 125 million years ago, the African Plate broke away from this region. When the African Plate broke away, forming the Atlantic Ocean, it left behind parts of the coasts of Massachusetts and Maine.

Some 17,000 years ago, the last glacier released its grip. It left its handiwork everywhere—in thousands of lakes and ponds, *moraines*, marshes, sand plains, bare rock surfaces, and rubble mounds called *drumlins*. It also scattered millions of rocks torn loose from the bedrock across the land. Little coastal plain remains since the glaciers depressed the land while the sea levels rose as the glaciers melted. The plains were submerged.

From this violent activity came the region known today as New England. It is home to six states and over 13 million people. The coastline stretches some 6,130 miles (9,865 kilometers). The entire area includes nearly 72,000 square miles.

Student Activities

Answer the following questions based on the information in this selection.

1. Define the term *plate tectonics.* _____
   _____

2. When did the first impact of crustal plates occur in the area that is now New England? _____

3. After this collision, the Appalachians might have been as high as which mountain range today? _____
   What caused them to lose their height? _____

4. What was Pangaea? _____
   How did its formation affect the region of New England? _____
   _____

5. Which continental plate broke away, forming part of the coast of Maine and Massachusetts? _____
   This break began the formation of which ocean? _____

6. Why is there very little coastal plain in New England? _____
   _____

Complete the following activities.

7. Use a variety of resource books to do additional research and prepare a report on plate tectonics. Include information about the uplifting and erosion of mountains. As part of the report, use an outline map of the world to draw and label the major plates. Share the information you gained with other members of the class.

8. Use the following activity to demonstrate the movement of the plates across the earth's surface over the centuries. Cut out the shapes of the present continents from an outline map of the world. Using reference books such as atlases and other geography books, try to put the continents together to form the super continent, Pangaea. Paste your model on blue construction paper. Next, cut out additional shapes of the continents and glue to blue construction paper to illustrate the movement of the plates at various stages to their current positions.

9. Use clay to build models of plates and demonstrate how the Appalachian Mountains could have been uplifted during the collision of the European, African, and North American plates.

Life in New England

New England was known for its proud, independent Yankee farmers in the 1800s. At that time, more than half the land was used for crops or pasture. Today, with most New Englanders working in light industry and the hilly fields not suited for mechanized farming, only about 12 percent of New England's land is used for farming. Because of *reforestation* efforts, the forests are once again covering nearly four fifths of the area. However, farming still continues to be strong in many areas, especially the Connecticut River Valley. Farmers here produce a variety of crops, including tobacco, apples, and other fruit. In addition, Maine is well-known for the potato, Vermont ships milk to other areas, Massachusetts and New Hampshire export apples, and maple syrup flows from New Hampshire and Vermont. The swampy Cape Cod *lowlands* grow about 60 percent of all the cranberries produced in the United States.

From the time of the early settlers, many New Englanders turned to occupations such as fishing, shipping, and forest products. Coastal New England served as the center for the whaling industry in the eighteenth century. At the same time, the shallow waters off the coast provided a very productive fishing ground. Boston, Portland, New Bedford, and Gloucester became the chief ports for the fishing fleets. Softwood forests were a valuable resource until their numbers were depleted by clearing land for farming and shipbuilding. The most abundant mining resource was granite. It is found in Massachusetts, Vermont, New Hampshire, and Maine. Vermont is also noted for marble and asbestos.

Only small amounts of coal were available for fuel, but the streams tumbling out of the hills could turn the water wheel. The water wheel in turn could provide the power for mills along the rivers of New England. These small factories made this region the first industrial area in the United States. Small industries producing *textiles*, shoes, clocks, and small arms began to cover the region. By the twentieth century, these industries began to decline and move to other areas of the nation. New England's new industrial concentration has been in high-technology industries such as computers, machine tools, aircraft engines, and precision instruments. Industrial activity today focuses on Boston and smaller, neighboring cities of southern New England.

While a solid core of New Englanders still trace their roots to England, there have been massive influxes of Irish, Italians, and French Canadians, along with Germans, Portuguese, African Americans, East Europeans, and others. Boston, which was started as a Puritan city, is now half Roman Catholic. The cities often have distinctive cultural districts that help to provide the *multicultural* atmosphere.

New England provides scenic areas, cultural experiences, and historical treasures for the tourist. In fact, tourism has become a multibillion-dollar business in this region. From the Pilgrims at Plymouth and the celebration of the first Thanksgiving to the opening shots of the American Revolution at Lexington and Concord, the history student will find the nation's history deeply rooted in New England. Those tourists who enjoy nature can climb to the top of Mount Washington, the scene of some of North America's fiercest storms, or enjoy the tranquility of a village green, where white churches and houses stand as they have for generations. New England continues to be a popular tourist attraction.

Student Activities

Answer each of the following questions based on the information you just read about the human characteristics of New England.

1. The percentage of land used for farming in New England today is about _____. What two factors have brought about this reduction in the amount of farming?

   _____

   _____

2. What river valley is the best-known farming area of New England? _____ What crops are grown there? _____

3. How did swiftly flowing rivers and streams help to change the way people in New England made a living? _____

4. After the small industries of New England began to decline, the area began a new industrial concentration. What is this new concentration? _____

   _____

   Do you feel these industries provide a promising outlook for the future of New England's economy? Why or why not? _____

Complete the following activities.

1. New England has been described as an example of a reforestation project that has worked. Research the concept of reforestation. What is reforestation and how is it carried out? Find proof of its success in New England.

2. Research the concept of the water wheel providing power for a small factory. Make a series of drawings or build a model of such a factory to explain how the water is used for energy.

Inventors of New England

The *Industrial Revolution* in the United States had its beginning in Great Britain in the late 1700s. Steam engines powered by coal helped to transform the British countryside into areas of blast furnaces and mills. After the War of 1812, the United States became a major consumer of British goods and a source of raw materials.

One of the raw materials supplied to Great Britain was cotton. However, the task of handpicking cotton bolls was hard and tedious. It was a New Englander, Eli Whitney, who stepped in to invent the cotton gin. Whitney was born in 1765 in Massachusetts. He showed an early talent for fixing things and opened his own nail company.

After graduating from Yale, he moved to Georgia to begin a teaching career. He saw the inefficiency of handpicking cotton and started working with his tools. By 1794, he had secured financial backing and a patent and began manufacturing the cotton gin. Not only did he revolutionize the cotton industry, but he returned to New England where he continued to contribute to the industrialization of the United States. One of his ideas included developing products with *interchangeable parts*. He received a government contract that allowed him to develop arms with interchangeable parts in the first mass-production plant located at New Haven, Connecticut.

Whitney was only one of the many inventors in the New England area who helped to bring the Industrial Revolution to full force in the United States. In 1793, Slater Mill, established in Pawtucket, Rhode Island, became the first textile factory in the nation. Twenty years later, Francis Cabot Lowell developed the first American power loom and installed it in the first *integrated textile factory*. For the first time, power looms were used and combined the spinning of the yarn and the weaving of cloth.

Other outstanding inventors from the New England area helped to develop such items as the steel plow, elevators, vulcanized rubber, the telegraph, and the first transatlantic telegraph cable. Each invention helped to ensure that the United States would take the lead in the Industrial Revolution and maintain that leadership in the world. Many of the products we take for granted today can be traced back to the inventive spirit of the early New Englanders.

Name _____

Student Activities

New England has served as home to many inventors and their inventions that helped to change the economy of the entire nation. This chart shows some of these inventors and their contributions.

Inventor	Location	Date	Invention
Eli Whitney	Westborough, Massachusetts	1793	
Francis Cabot Lowell	Waltham, Massachusetts	1813	
Elisha G. Otis	Halifax, Vermont	1852	
John Deere	Rutland, Vermont	1837	
Charles Goodyear	New Haven, Connecticut	1839	
Samuel F. B. Morse	Charlestown, Massachusetts	1837	
Cyrus Field	Stockbridge, Massachusetts	1858	
Alexander Graham Bell	Boston, Massachusetts	1876	

Complete the following activities based on the information provided in the chart above.

1. Using research books and your text, complete the chart above by finding the major contribution made by each of the inventors listed.

2. Construct a time line for the period of history covering 1790 to 1900. Stretch a piece of yarn across a bulletin board or the wall. Divide the yarn into 12 equal sections representing the decades from 1790 to 1900. Indicate the decades by writing their dates (1790, 1800, etc.) on narrow strips of construction paper and attaching them to the time line. On a note card (3" x 5"), write the name of each inventor and the date and name of the invention. Attach these cards to the time line.

3. Research the period of history (1790-1900) for major events that occurred. Write these events on pieces of colored construction paper (3" x 5") and attach them to the time line.

4. Choose one of these inventors, or another if you wish, and research his or her life. Prepare a three-minute monologue role-playing that inventor, telling your story to the class.

5. Research to find other inventors who lived in New England and add them to the time line.

The New England States

New England is a small region in the northeast corner of the United States that is known for picturesque rural villages, numerous fishing villages, and beautiful autumn scenery. It was the nation's first industrial center, and manufacturing is still an important part of the region.

The region is composed of six states—Connecticut, Maine, Massachusetts, New Hampshire, Rhode Island, and Vermont. The total population of this region is about 13 million, about five percent of the nation's total. The states are relatively small in area compared to states from other regions. Maine, the largest New England state, has three times the area of the next largest state but ranks only thirty-ninth in area in the nation. Rhode Island is the smallest state in the United States.

The New England States

State	Capital	Date of Statehood	Population	Area (Sq. Mi.)	Rank in Size
Connecticut	Hartford	1788	3,295,669	5,006	48
Maine	Augusta	1820	1,239,448	33,127	39
Massachusetts	Boston	1788	6,012,268	8,262	45
New Hampshire	Concord	1788	1,123,310	9,283	44
Rhode Island	Providence	1790	1,000,012	1,213	50
Vermont	Montpelier	1791	575,691	9,615	43

Student Activities

Using the information in the chart above, answer the following questions.

1. Based on the population data above, what was the total population of the New England States? _____

2. Calculate the percentage of the population of New England made up by each state:
   Connecticut _____   Maine _____
   Massachusetts_____   New Hampshire _____
   Rhode Island_____   Vermont _____

3. What is the total area of New England in square miles? _____

4. List the New England States below in order by area from the largest to the smallest.
   1. _____   4. _____
   2. _____   5. _____
   3. _____   6. _____

5. Which two of the New England States were not part of the original colonies?
   _____   _____

   Research to find to which colonies they belonged. _____

6. On the map on the previous page, label each state and capital city. Use the following colors to complete the map:
   Connecticut—Yellow   Maine—Red
   Rhode Island—Green   Massachusetts—Blue
   New Hampshire—Orange   Vermont—Brown

The Middle Atlantic States

Goals for This Unit

Students will

1. use atlases to find the absolute and relative location of sites in the Middle Atlantic States.
2. define and investigate the concept of *megalopolis* and explain how urbanization is affecting rural areas.
3. identify the key physical characteristics of the Middle Atlantic States.
4. use charts to help identify how people in the Middle Atlantic States make a living.
5. construct a model showing the route of the Appalachian Trail.
6. validate facts known about the history of Washington, D.C., and research major monuments and buildings.

Rationale

The Middle Atlantic States region forms one of the most populous areas of the United States. The major ports and harbors make it a center for immigration and trade. Many immigrants have received their first view of the United States from a ship passing the Statue of Liberty and heading into the New York Harbor. It has also become the financial center of the nation. The stock exchanges and the headquarters of many major banks are located in New York City. The region also contains Washington, D.C., the capital of the United States. Headquarters for all major branches of the federal government are located in the capital city. The Middle Atlantic States region continues to be a vibrant, expanding area of the nation.

Skills Taught in This Unit	
using atlases	using latitude and longitude grids
reading and labeling maps	interpreting charts
calculating percentages	collecting data
constructing models	role-playing
making map keys	

Vocabulary

plain	coastal plain	moraine deposits
estuary	Piedmont	fall line
Appalachian Highlands	velocity	megalopolis
metropolitan	Andrew Ellicott	Pierre L'Enfant
Appalachian Trail	Benjamin Banneker	

Background Information

The Middle Atlantic States region is composed of the states of New York, Delaware, Pennsylvania, Maryland, and New Jersey. In this unit, the five themes of geography will be applied to the study of these states. The region is a vibrant one that houses the nation's capital as well as the largest city in the United States. The region is especially noted for its growing urban areas.

Location in the Middle Atlantic States

Themes of Geography: Location, Place, Movement, Region

This activity provides the absolute location of the Middle Atlantic States and their major cities. Students will need to understand how to read an atlas and use the lines of latitude and longitude prior to completing this activity. Students accompany two travelers as they tour the Middle Atlantic States and are asked to identify the cities visited by using degrees of latitude and longitude.

Objectives
Students will
1. discuss the meaning of absolute location and how to locate a position on the earth using the grids on maps.
2. complete the blanks in a travel story by using an atlas to identify the cities.

Materials: classroom atlases, pencils, paper, "Location in the Middle Atlantic States" activity sheets

Procedure
1. Discuss in class the meaning of absolute location and the grid system of latitude and longitude. A review of reading the grids of latitude and longitude on a map may be necessary before assigning this activity.
2. Students are to read the story "The Adventures of Don and Gail" and fill in the blanks by writing either the name of the city or the degrees of latitude and longitude that would identify the city.
3. Students may check their work by sharing with a partner.
4. Ask students to plan a trip they would like to take and write about it in the same way this story was written. They should then trade stories with a partner to find out where their partner would be traveling.

Physical Features of the Middle Atlantic States

Themes of Geography: Location, Place, Region

The Middle Atlantic States share many common physical features. This activity looks at the region as a whole and identifies these major features. Several important geographic terms are introduced in this section.

Objectives
Students will
1. study geographic terms describing the physical features of the Middle Atlantic States and match the terms with correct definitions.
2. label a map of the Middle Atlantic States showing the major physical features.

Materials: resource books, atlases, colored pencils, pencil, "Physical Features of the Middle Atlantic States" activity sheets

Procedure
1. Discuss in class the meaning of physical features. Ask students to make a list of examples of physical features as opposed to human features.
2. Read in class the "Physical Features of the Middle Atlantic States" activity sheets. Ask students to make a list of physical features they identify as the selection is read.
3. Compile a class list of the physical features identified by individual students.
4. Students should complete the first activity, filling in the geographic terms to match the definitions provided.
5. Students should label the map of the Middle Atlantic States and use the color key to shade the map with colored pencils.

A Megalopolis

Themes of Geography: Place, Movement, Human-Environment Interaction, Region

A *megalopolis* is a region made of up two or more metropolitan areas. The northern Atlantic Coast of the United States houses a megalopolis that stretches from Washington, D.C., to Boston, Massachusetts. The major cities located here have metropolitan areas so large that in some points the areas nearly meet. The growth of urban areas has been occurring all over the world. Nowhere is this better demonstrated than in this megalopolis.

Objectives
Students will
1. read maps and charts to gain an understanding of the term *megalopolis*.
2. use information from charts to help solve problems dealing with population and percentages.
3. make a travel brochure for one of the major cities in the megalopolis.
4. label and color a map of the megalopolis.

Materials: colored pencils, calculators, reference books, white drawing paper, pencils, crayons, markers, "A Megalopolis" activity sheets

Procedure
1. Introduce the term *megalopolis* to the class. Ask students to brainstorm for examples of a megalopolis. List examples on the board or on chart paper.
2. Read the information given in "A Megalopolis" activity sheets. Students should then complete the activities in Part I. These questions serve as a review of the material just read. Discuss the answers in class.

3. Students should then complete activity 1, using the information provided in the chart. Calculators may be used in this activity.
4. The second activity asks students to label and color the "Megalopolis" map. Students should be encouraged to use colored pencils for any map work.
5. Resource books will be needed for the third activity. Students need to research each city to find points that interest them. They should share this information by creating travel brochures. A variety of art materials such as crayons, colored chalk, and white drawing paper should be available for student use. After students share their brochures with the class, display them on a bulletin board.

The Appalachian Trail

Themes of Geography: Place, Human-Environment Interaction, Movement, Region

The Appalachian Trail is a mountain-hiking footpath that runs along the crest of the Appalachian Mountains in the eastern United States. The trail extends more than 2,000 miles from Georgia to Maine. The trail forms a backbone that extends across the Middle Atlantic States. The Appalachian Trail provides recreational opportunities for people from around the world.

Objectives
Students will
1. label a map showing the states through which the Appalachian Trail runs.
2. work with a partner to plan for a trip across the Appalachian Trail.
3. construct a model of the Appalachian Trail.

Materials: clay, outline maps of the eastern United States, pieces of cardboard, colored pencils, paper, pencils, "The Appalachian Trail" activity sheets

Procedure
1. Discuss in class the activity of mountain-hiking. Brainstorm a list of materials that might be necessary for such an activity.
2. Read "The Appalachian Trail" activity sheets. Use a wall map to show the route taken by the trail. Students should then complete activities 1 and 2 by labeling the map on the activity sheets. Coloring the map is optional.
3. Ask students to choose a partner for the third activity. Partners should work together to role-play a planned hike of the entire Appalachian Trail. They should list what they would take with them and what they would need to do to prepare for such a trip. Each group should report its plans to the class.
4. The final activity, constructing a model of the Appalachian Trail, could be done individually or as a group activity. Students will need an outline map of the eastern United States. The size may vary, depending on how the activity will be carried out. The outline map should be pasted onto a piece of cardboard. Students will then use clay to form a ridge following the path of the Appalachian Trail through the 14 states. Students may wish to label some of the mountains that are crossed along the way.

Washington, D.C., The National Capital

Themes of Geography: Location, Place, Human-Environment Interaction, Movement, Region

The Middle Atlantic States region includes the site of Washington, D.C. While it is not part of any state, the District of Columbia is located between Maryland and Virginia. Since the city is on the eastern shore of the Potomac River, it is usually grouped with the Middle Atlantic States. Washington, D.C., is one of the few cities in the world that was planned before it was built. It continues to be a city that houses the government of the United States of America.

Objectives

Students will

1. read a brief history of the city of Washington, D.C.
2. develop a map key identifying major monuments and buildings in downtown Washington.
3. write a report on one of the major monuments or buildings in downtown Washington, D.C.

Materials: reference books, pencil, paper, "Washington, D.C., The National Capital" activity sheets

Procedure

1. Ask the class to share facts they already know or believe they know about Washington, D.C. List all facts on the board or on chart paper.
2. Read "Washington, D.C, The National Capital" activity sheets. During the discussion of what was read, add to the facts on the board. Also check to see whether any of the facts were incorrect and need to be deleted.
3. Students should then complete Part I as a review of the information read. Go over the questions after they have been answered.
4. Students should use reference books to help complete Part II. They should list the name of each monument or building beside the number that represents it on the map.
5. Students may choose their favorite monument or building to research. If drawing paper is used, the drawing may be placed at the top of the paper and the report written below it. After sharing their work with the class, display the work on the wall or bulletin board.
6. Refer to the list of information gathered at the beginning of this lesson. Make certain that all the facts have been verified. If some of them need further research, ask students to check on the validity of the statements. Use the list as a review of what was learned about Washington, D.C.

Conclusion

From Washington, D.C., to New York City, the urban areas of the Middle Atlantic States continue to grow. The rural areas, while growing smaller, are also vital in the production of agricultural products. The Middle Atlantic States region provides important goods and services that are vital to the welfare of the entire nation. These states have a diverse population that must work to better understand each other, while continuing the work of economic growth and development. Many challenges are ahead for this region of the country.

Location in the Middle Atlantic States

The Middle Atlantic States region is made up of these five states: New York, Pennsylvania, New Jersey, Delaware, and Maryland. This region stretches between 38° N and 45° N latitude. It lies between 72° W and 82° W longitude. By using the degrees of latitude and longitude, it is possible to pinpoint a location on the face of the earth.

Directions: Use an atlas and the degrees of latitude and longitude to solve the following problems. Read the story and fill in the blanks either with the name of the appropriate city by using its coordinates as clues or by finding the appropriate coordinates for the city.

The Adventures of Don and Gail

Don and Gail traveled across the Middle Atlantic States during their summer vacation. They traveled from their home in _____ (**40° 25' N, 79° 55' W**) east on Interstate 76 to Breezewood and then turned east onto Interstate 70. This part of their trip took them into the state of Maryland and to the city of _____ (**39° 18' N, 76° 37' W**). After touring the Inner Harbor and the National Aquarium, they visited Fort McHenry, where the national anthem was written. Then they headed south on Interstate 95 to the city of _____ (**38° 52' N, 77° W**). Here they toured the National Zoo and rode the Metro. Don and Gail were thrilled to see how their national government worked.

Once again they traveled north on Interstate 95 around the city of Baltimore and into the state of Delaware to the city of **Wilmington** (_____). Here they visited the Old Swedes Church and the Delaware Art Museum. Don and Gail were both surprised to learn that Swedish settlers founded the first permanent colony in Delaware. After exploring the northern part of Delaware, our travelers decided to venture north on Interstate 95 once again. They soon found themselves entering the state of Pennsylvania.

Their next stop was the city of _____ (**40° N, 75° 10' W**). Here Don and Gail spent three days visiting famous historic sites. Gail was particularly delighted to see the Liberty Bell. She had read many stories about this famous bell that rang to announce the signing of the Declaration of Independence. Don enjoyed the tour of Independence Hall where the Declaration of Independence was written. They both agreed that the early history of their country seemed to come alive as they strolled along the streets of this beautiful city.

After their three-day stay, Don and Gail decided to cross the Delaware River and take the New Jersey Turnpike north to Interstate 195. Then they turned west until they came to the city of _____ (**40° 15' N, 74° 41' W**). Here again they found reminders of the American Revolution. They toured the Old Barracks where George Washington led an attack on the Hessian Soldiers (German soldiers fighting for England in the American Revolution) and defeated them on Christmas Day in 1776. After the tour of the Barracks, Don and Gail toured the Capitol building.

Their next stop in New Jersey took them farther north on the New Jersey Turnpike to the city of **Newark** (_____). This is the largest city in New Jersey. Here our travelers visited the New Jersey Historical Society Museum and the Cathedral of the Sacred Heart and First Presbyterian Church completed in 1791.

After visiting Newark, Don and Gail traveled approximately ten miles east to the city of _____ (**40° 45' N, 74° W**). Their first trip was to see the Statue of Liberty. They enjoyed seeing the beautiful lady with her lamp held high, welcoming all to the United States. Then they headed for the United Nations building to see where delegates from around the world meet to discuss issues and work for international peace. Don also insisted that they go to the top of the Empire State Building to view the nation's largest city. Time seemed to fly as the two toured the sites of the city and saw two plays on Broadway. After a week in the city, Don and Gail continued their trip by going north on Interstate 87 along the Hudson River.

Their trip north took them past West Point and the United States Military Academy. There they toured the West Point Museum and the Cadet Chapel. Next they spent time in scenic Kingston, where they discovered the Senate House and Museum and the Old Dutch Church. Their journey finally brought them to the city of **Albany** (_____). In Albany, Don and Gail visited the state capitol and the New York State Museum. They also explored the Schuyler Mansion and Historic Cherry Hill.

From Albany, Don and Gail took Interstate 90 west along the Erie canal. They arrived in the city of **Syracuse** (_____) in time to visit the Lowe Art Center at Syracuse University. The next morning they visited the Canal Museum before continuing on their trip. Again traveling west, they arrived in the city of _____ (**42° 55' N, 78° 50' W**). Here they saw the Museum of Science, the Theodore Roosevelt Inaugural National Historic Site, and the Zoological Gardens. The following day they took a side trip to Niagara Falls to view both the American and Canadian Falls. This was Don's first trip into Canada.

After leaving Buffalo, Don and Gail continued west on Interstate 90 along Lake Erie. They entered Pennsylvania and found themselves in the city of _____ (**42° 10' N, 80° 7' W**). Here they visited the USS *Niagara*, Oliver Perry's flagship, used to defeat the British on Lake Erie during the War of 1812.

Finally, Don and Gail traveled south on Interstate 79 back to their home in Pittsburgh. This trip will be one that they will always remember.

Physical Features of the Middle Atlantic States

One of the most important features of the Middle Atlantic region is the Atlantic Coastal Plain. A *plain* is a wide area of flat or gently rolling land. A *coastal plain* is a plain that is bordered by a large body of water. The Atlantic Coastal Plain extends through all the Middle Atlantic States. It is flat and remains close to sea level, even inland.

One interesting feature of the coastal plain is Long Island. The island was deposited off the New York coast by ice sheets during the last ice age. It is actually a series of rock, gravel, and sand deposits, called *moraine deposits,* that are separated from the mainland by Long Island Sound. It extends about 120 miles (190 kilometers) from the mouth of the Hudson River into the Atlantic Ocean. Agriculture and fishing are still important in the eastern part of Long Island. The island has experienced enormous urban and suburban growth since World War II.

The coastal plain also features the coastal estuaries. An *estuary* is a water passage formed where rivers meet seawater. Chesapeake Bay, in Maryland and Virginia, is the largest bay on the Atlantic coast of the United States. It is about 200 miles (320 kilometers) long from north to south and from 3 to 25 miles (5 to 40 kilometers) wide. The bay is a shipping artery with major ports at Norfolk, Virginia, and Baltimore, Maryland. It is a major supplier of fish and shellfish, but pollution has begun to threaten the industry in recent years. The Delaware Bay, which separates Delaware and New Jersey, forms another estuary. The Delaware estuary is about 12 miles wide (19 kilometers) where it joins the Atlantic. A smaller estuary is at the mouth of the Hudson River in New York City. All three estuaries provide natural harbors that are ice-free all winter.

Inland from the Atlantic Coastal Plain is the *Piedmont* region. Here gently sloping hills connect the Coastal Plain and the Appalachian Mountains. Where the Piedmont and the Atlantic Coastal Plains meet, rivers plunge over the *fall line.* The fall line marks the furthest point in each river navigable by ships, because of the higher elevation of the land and numerous waterfalls. Because of available water power, many cities have grown in this region.

The *Appalachian Highlands* rise westward from the Piedmont. They run through the Middle Atlantic States in a northeast-southwest direction. In this region, the mountains are made up of folded parallel ridges and valleys. According to the theory of plate tectonics, they were created over 300 million years ago when eastern North America collided with Africa. Included in the Appalachian ranges are the Adirondacks in New York and the Blue Ridge Mountains that begin in southern Pennsylvania.

Major rivers cut through the Appalachians as they run to the Atlantic. The Hudson River flows south through the Appalachian Mountains in New York. Where the Hudson meets the Mohawk River, the city of Albany has grown. The Susquehanna River flows south from New York through Pennsylvania and empties into Chesapeake Bay. It is the largest North American river flowing into the Atlantic Ocean. Other major rivers in this region include the Potomac and Delaware.

During the last ice age, glaciers covered much of the north part of this region. The Adirondack Mountains were eroded by ice sheets. The Finger Lakes in western New York were carved by glaciers. Two Great Lakes—Ontario and Erie—(also formed by glaciers) help to form the border between Canada and the United States in this region.

Student Activities

Part I. Complete the following activity by filling in the blanks with the correct answers from the selection just read. Place one letter in each blank.

1. Wide areas of flat or gently rolling land   _ _ ◯ _ _ _

2. A plain bordered by a large body of water   ◯ _ _ _ _ _ _
   _ _ _ _ _

3. Rock, gravel, and sand deposits   _ _ _ ◯ _ _

4. Island deposited off coast of New York by glaciers   ◯ _ _   _ _ _ ◯ _ _

5. Region of sloping hills between coastal plain and mountains   ◯ _ _ _ _ _ _

6. Line where the Piedmont meets the coastal plain   _ _ _   _ _ ◯ _

7. Water passage formed where rivers meet seawater   _ _ _ _ ◯ _ _

8. Western New York lakes carved by glaciers   _ _ _ _ _ _   _ ◯ _ _

9. Largest bay on Atlantic coast of the United States   _ ◯ _ _ ◯ _ _ _ _   _ _ _

10. Unscramble the letters circled above to name the mountain range running through the Middle Atlantic States.

_ _ _ _ _ _ _ _ _ _ _

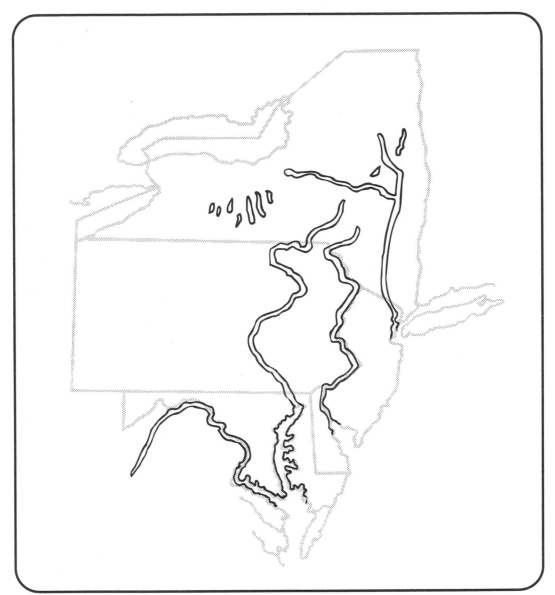

Part II. Use the map above to complete the following activities.

1. Label the following physical features on the map above:

Lakes	Rivers	Bays
Lake Ontario	Susquehanna	Delaware
Lake Erie	Hudson	Chesapeake
Finger Lakes	Potomac	New York
	Delaware	

2. Color the map with colored pencils using the following key:

Delaware—yellow	New York—red
Maryland—orange	Pennsylvania—green
New Jersey—purple	Atlantic Ocean—blue

A Megalopolis

A *megalopolis* is a region made up of two or more metropolitan areas. A *metropolitan* area consists of a central city that has a population of at least 50,000 and the suburbs that surround the city. Metropolitan areas form a megalopolis when they attract enough people and industry to expand and begin to grow together.

The largest megalopolis in the United States includes the areas of Boston, New York City, Philadelphia, Baltimore, and Washington, D.C. This area extends approximately 600 miles from Massachusetts to northern Virginia. There are about 42 million people living in this area.

Boston is the capital city of Massachusetts and the largest city in the New England region. It is New England's leading business, financial, government, and transportation center. Boston is known as the Cradle of Liberty because it was the birthplace of the American Revolution.

New York City serves as the center of the megalopolis and is the largest city in the United States. New York City began as a trading post established by Henry Hudson in 1609. Today, it is a major seaport and railway center and handles nearly 40 percent of the nation's air traffic. New York is known as the financial and commercial center of the nation because of the stock exchanges, large numbers of corporate headquarters, and many banks located there. It is important to the world because it serves as home to the United Nations. The population of the New York City area has expanded eastward across Long Island, northward into Connecticut, and westward across the Hudson River into New Jersey.

The second major Atlantic seaport is Philadelphia. Its location on the lower Delaware River provides access to the Atlantic Ocean through the Delaware Bay. Philadelphia was planned by William Penn in 1682. It served as the national capital from 1790 to 1800. The Declaration of Independence was written and signed in Philadelphia. Today Philadelphia is a major manufacturing, banking, and educational center. The urban area of Philadelphia has spread westward into Pennsylvania and eastward into New Jersey.

Baltimore, Maryland's largest city, is located on the western shore of the Chesapeake Bay. About half of the population of Maryland lives in the metropolitan area of Baltimore. The city has one of the largest natural harbors in the world. It is the only United States port with two links to the Atlantic Ocean. The Chesapeake-Delaware Canal provides a link to the north and the Chesapeake Bay provides a southern link. The city was founded in 1729 by the Maryland legislature. Today, Baltimore is a major manufacturing center with over 2,000 factories. The industries range from steel manufacturing and the production of electronic equipment to the largest production of spices and seasonings in the world.

Washington, D.C., has a unique status among cities in the United States because it is not a part of any state. The city was built to be the national capital on land ceded by Maryland and Virginia for the capital district. The District of Columbia was designed in 1789 by French engineer and architect, *Pierre L'Enfant.* Today, Washington, D.C. is the headquarters of the United States Government. The president of the United States, the members of Congress, the Supreme Court justices, and about 370,000 other federal government employees work in the city.

Student Activities

Part I. Use the map below and the information from the material you just read to answer the review questions.

Megalopolis

1. Name the state or district that is home to each of the cities shown on the map.

   Boston _____   New York City _____

   Philadelphia _____   Baltimore _____

   Washington _____

2. Each of these cities is a major port on which ocean? _____

3. The largest city which forms the center of the megalopolis is _____.

4. The only United States port with two entrances to the Atlantic Ocean is_____.

5. The United Nations is located in the city of _____.

6. William Penn planned this city, which was home to the signing of the Declaration of Independence. _____

7. The Cradle of the American Revolution is the nickname of the city of _____ because _____.

8. Define *megalopolis.*_____

9. Define *metropolitan area.* _____

City	Founded	Population	Area
Baltimore	1729	736,014	80 sq. mi.
Boston	1630	574,283	46 sq. mi.
New York City	1609	7,322,564	301 sq. mi.
Philadelphia	1682	1,585,577	136 sq. mi.
Washington, D.C.	1790	606,900	61 sq. mi.

Part II. Complete each of the following activities.

1. Use the table above to answer the questions below.

   a. Name the smallest city in population and area. _____

   b. The area of New York City is approximately six times that of which city?_____

   _____

   c. How many years older is New York City than Washington, D.C.? _____

   d. What is the total population of these cities?_____

   e. Based on the total population, what percent of the people live in each city?

   Baltimore _____   Boston _____

   New York City _____   Philadelphia _____

   Washington _____

   f. What is the total area (square miles) included in these cities?_____

   g. How many times more people does New York City have than Boston?_____

2. Use the map of the megalopolis to complete the following:

   a. Label the Atlantic Ocean and color it blue.

   b. Label each state containing one of the cities named in the chart above and color it yellow.

   c. Label all other states and color them brown.

3. Research one of the major cities in the megalopolis and design a travel brochure for that city. Include information that would make tourists want to visit the city. Information about interesting sites and activities should be included. Share your brochure with the class.

The Appalachian Trail

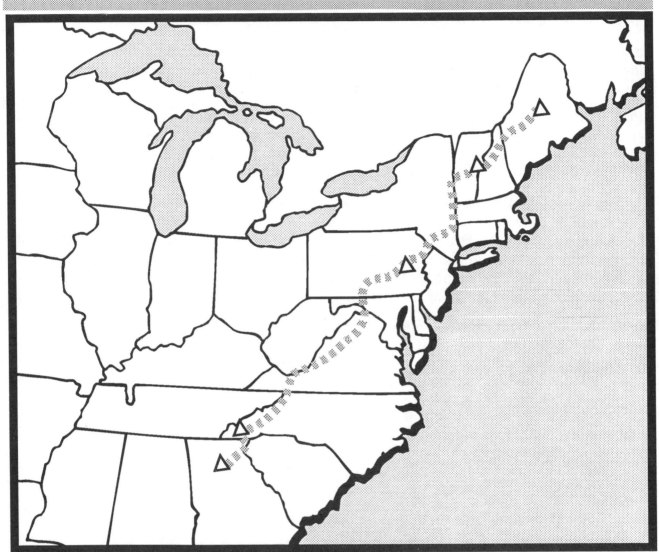

The *Appalachian Trail* is a mountain hiking footpath along the crests of the Appalachian Mountains in the eastern United States that is more than 2,000 miles (3,200 kilometers) long. It follows the Appalachian Mountains from Georgia to Maine. The trail passes through 14 states, two national parks, and eight national forests. The trail was completed, except for minor alterations, in 1937. In 1968 it was designated a national scenic trail. The trail is marked and maintained by hiking groups under the supervision of the Appalachian Trail Conference headquartered in Harpers Ferry, West Virginia.

The southwestern end of the trail is at Springer Mountain in Georgia. Springer Mountain rises to 3,820 feet (1,164 meters). From Springer Mountain the trail runs through forests of beech and oak trees as it winds its way to the Great Smoky Mountains. These mountains stretch along the border of Tennessee and North Carolina. The highest peak on the trail is at Clingman's Dome in Tennessee. This peak reaches 6,642 feet (2,025 meters) above sea level.

As the trail stretches along the Tennessee and North Carolina boundary, hikers see Mount Mitchell in the distance. Mount Mitchell is the highest peak in the Appalachian Mountains, reaching 61,682 feet (2,037 meters). Mount Mitchell is located in the Blue Ridge Mountains of North Carolina.

The longest stretch of the trail runs through the state of Virginia. Here the trail goes along the Allegheny Mountains and the Blue Ridge. At one point, it follows the boundary between Virginia and West Virginia.

In Pennsylvania, the trail goes over Hawk Mountain. Hawk Mountain is a favorite spot for bird watchers. Many hawks are seen soaring past this mountain. The trail then runs east from Pennsylvania into New Jersey and New York. The mountains are not as high here, but there are many hilly, wooded areas of great beauty.

From New York, the trail goes across Connecticut and into the Berkshire Mountains of Massachusetts. From there, it reaches into the Green Mountains of Vermont, a favorite skiing area in the winter. From Vermont, the path leads through the White Mountains of New Hampshire and up to the peak of Mount Washington. This peak is known for sudden storms and wind velocity. The greatest wind *velocity* (speed) ever measured, 231 miles (370 kilometers) per hour, was on this mountain.

The trail runs from New Hampshire into western Maine. From the trail, many miles of forests and lakes are visible. The trail ends at Mount Katahdin in central Maine. Mount Katahdin stands at 5,267 feet (1,605 meters). Mount Katahdin is said to be the first place in the United States that is touched by rays of the rising sun in the morning.

Student Activities

Complete each of the following activities.

1. Label each of the 14 states that the Appalachian Trail travels through on the map on the preceding page. Use postal abbreviations.

2. Label each of the following mountains on the map.
   a. Springer Mountain   d. Hawk Mountain
   b. Clingman's Dome   e. Mount Washington
   c. Mount Katahdin

3. Role-play that you were going to hike the Appalachian Trail. Hiking the entire trail takes between three and four months. Work with a partner to decide what you would need to take with you on your trip. Include in your discussion what clothing would be needed and what supplies would be taken. Remember that everything you take will have to be carried in a backpack. Include in your discussion the time of year you will be making the trip. Be prepared to share your plans with the rest of the class.

4. Construct a model of the Appalachian Trail. Begin with an outline map on cardboard of the eastern United States. Create the Appalachian Highlands out of clay. Then, mark the route followed by the trail through the mountains.

Washington, D.C.
The National Capital

Washington, D.C., the capital of the United States of America, was named in honor of George Washington. The D.C. stands for District of Columbia. The land that makes up the District of Columbia was given by Virginia and Maryland for the capital city. Washington, D.C., is the only American city that is not a part of any state. It is situated along the east bank of the Potomac River.

During the early years of the United States, Congress met in a different city almost every time it met. Soon there became a need for one permanent capital. However, every state wanted such a city. Alexander Hamilton and Thomas Jefferson helped to reach a compromise that would locate the city on federal land not belonging to any state. Further compromise between northern and southern states located the city between the two regions.

Washington is one of the few cities in the world designed before it was built. It was the first city to be created specifically to become the capital of a country. President George Washington chose the site in 1791, and hired *Pierre L'Enfant*, a French engineer, to draw up plans for the city. A commission was formed and the task of surveying the land and establishing boundaries went to *Andrew Ellicott* and *Benjamin Banneker*.

L'Enfant lived by the philosophy "Make no little plans." He drew up plans for the city on a very large scale that would leave room for future growth and development. The highest point in the area, Jenkin's Hill, became the site for the new Capitol. The President's Palace would be located one mile away, with a good view of the Potomac River. The two would be linked by Pennsylvania Avenue. Just south of the President's Palace would be a mall that would extend east and west back to the Capitol. L'Enfant's plan called for a combination of two street patterns: the rectangular blocks typical of many American cities and the wide, radiating boulevards of his native capital, Paris. A system of broad avenues would radiate from the Capitol in all directions like the spokes of a wheel. Parks, statues, and monuments were important parts of the city's layout, which was designed to provide a grand view of the monuments and government buildings. The plans L'Enfant drew established the pattern that would be set for the entire city. The Capitol would be the center of the city.

Contests were held to select the best design for the Capitol and the President's Palace. Dr. William Thornton, who was not a professional architect, submitted the winning design for the Capitol. James Hobin submitted the winning plan for the President's Palace. Both the buildings have been reconstructed, added to, and renovated as the need arose during the years.

The federal government moved to Washington, D.C., from Philadelphia in 1800. President John Adams and his Congress were the first to sit in the capital. In 1814, during the War of 1812, the British captured the city in retaliation for the capture and burning of York, the capital of Upper Canada. They burned the Capitol, the President's House, and other government buildings. Reconstruction of these buildings was completed in 1819. (The President's Palace became popularly known as the White House in the 1800s. However, it was not until 1901 that Theodore Roosevelt authorized White House as the official title.)

Today, Washington, D.C., has expanded to include large residential and business districts. The urban area has grown so large that it now spills over into the neighboring states of Virginia and Maryland. Thousands of people commute daily from their homes in the suburbs to their jobs in the District. Despite its growth, the main function of the city remains that of the government of the United States.

Student Activities

Part I. Complete each of the following statements, based on the material you just read about Washington, D.C.

1. The two states that gave land for the District of Columbia were _____ and _____.

2. What role did Alexander Hamilton and Thomas Jefferson play in helping to provide a permanent national capital? _____
_____

3. The winning design for the national capital was submitted by _____.

4. The federal government moved to Washington, D.C., from the city of _____ _____ in the year _____.

5. The major function of the city of Washington is the _____.

6. Washington, D.C., is located along the east bank of the _____ River.

7. The two men given the task of surveying the land and establishing the boundaries of the District of Columbia were _____ and _____.

8. The French engineer who drew up plans for the new city was _____.

9. L'Enfant developed a city plan which incorporated these two types of street patterns:
_____
_____

10. The Capitol and the White House are linked by _____ Avenue.

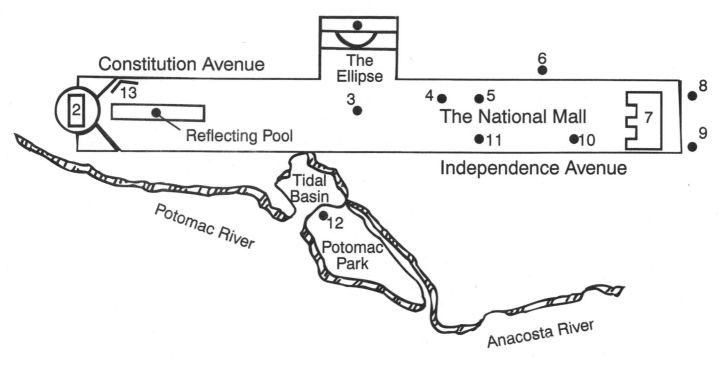

Constitution Avenue

The Ellipse

6

13

2

3

4 ● 5

The National Mall

8

7

Reflecting Pool

●11

●10

9

Independence Avenue

Tidal Basin

Potomac River

●12

Potomac Park

Anacosta River

Part II. Complete each of the following activities.

1. Thirteen important sites in downtown Washington are located on the map above. Use reference books to help prepare a key for the map. Write the appropriate name of the building or monument beside each of the numbers below. The names to use are Jefferson Memorial, Lincoln Memorial, Washington Monument, Vietnam Veterans Memorial, White House, United States Capitol, Supreme Court Building, Library of Congress, National Air and Space Museum, National Archives, National Museum of American History, National Museum of Natural History, and the Smithsonian Institution Building.

Key to Map of Washington, D.C.	
1. _____	8. _____
2. _____	9. _____
3. _____	10. _____
4. _____	11. _____
5. _____	12. _____
6. _____	13. _____
7. _____	

2. Research one of the monuments or buildings shown on the map above. Make a drawing of the site and write a brief report explaining why it is an attraction for visitors to the nation's capital.

The Southeast

Goals for This Unit

Students will

1. use atlases to find the absolute and relative location of sites in the Southeast.
2. construct a model of the Outer Banks of North Carolina.
3. identify and label the key physical features of the Southeast.
4. identify how people in the Southeast make a living and role-play the selection of a new manufacturing site.
5. use charts to explain the relationship between altitude and latitude and the weather in the Southeast.
6. investigate and compare the five largest urban areas in the Southeast.

Rationale

The study of the Southeast provides a view of a section of the United States that has undergone tremendous change. The Southeast is comprised of ten states, including Virginia, West Virginia, Kentucky, Tennessee, North Carolina, South Carolina, Georgia, Florida, Alabama, and Mississippi. This region is rich both in history and traditions, but it is also a rapidly growing area of the United States. The warm climate and inexpensive land helps to attract businesses from other parts of the United States and foreign countries. The once largely rural area has experienced the growth of urban areas throughout the region. States that once depended on "King Cotton" for their economic survival are now working to develop a diversified economy. The mixture of tradition and change provides challenges to the region that will require additional solutions in the coming years.

Skills Taught in This Unit	
using atlases	using latitude and longitude grids
reading and labeling maps	interpreting charts
collecting data	constructing models
role-playing	making a time line

Vocabulary

tidewater	fall line	monoculture
swamps	barrier islands	diversified agriculture
shoals	reefs	frost-free season
elevation	humid	hurricanes

Background Information

Ten states make up the region of the Southeast. The land region is dominated by coastal plains. Two large coastal plains include the Gulf Coastal Plain and the Atlantic Coastal Plain. The Appalachian Mountains also extend through the region from Maryland and West Virginia to Georgia. The region is bordered on the east by the Atlantic Ocean, on the north by the Ohio River and the state of Pennsylvania, on the south by the Gulf of Mexico, and on the west by the Mississippi River. The region has changed over the years from an economy based on cotton to one that is much more diversified. The region is rich in history and tradition, yet changing to meet the demands of the future.

Location in the Southeast

Themes of Geography: Location, Region

This activity involves students in using both absolute and relative location. *Absolute location* refers to using latitude and longitude to locate an exact site on a map. *Relative location* refers to giving the location of one site in relationship to another. These two tools allow students to gain an understanding of where places are in the Southeast.

Objectives

Students will

1. label a map giving the names of the Southeast states and their capitals.
2. use an atlas to give the absolute location of specified cities and to locate the names of cities when given the correct latitude and longitude.
3. use relative location clues to identify areas of the Southeast.

Materials: "Location in the Southeast" activity sheets, atlases, pencils

Procedure

1. Review both absolute and relative location with students.
2. Students should complete the first activity by placing both the capital and state next to the correct letter below the map.
3. The second and third activities require the use of a classroom atlas. Students may complete the activities individually or in small groups.
4. The final activity requires the use of relative location clues to identify specific sites. Students may need to use a map, atlas, or the text to assist them in finding the answers.

Physical Features of the Southeast

Themes of Geography: Place, Location, Region

The Southeast contains varied physical features. The Atlantic Coastal Plain extends from Virginia to Florida. The Gulf Coastal Plain extends westward from Florida to Mississippi. The Atlantic Coastal Plain then rises to the Piedmont and then the Appalachian Mountains. West of the Appalachians, the mountains give way to rolling hills and then part of the interior plain along the Mississippi River. Major streams and rivers also cut across the region. The activity will allow students to identify major physical features of the Southeast and correctly label them on a map.

Objectives
Students will
1. identify and define key terms relating to physical features in the Southeast.
2. label a map showing major physical features of the Southeast.

Materials: "Physical Features of the Southeast" activity sheets, pencils, colored pencils, atlases, textbooks

Procedure
1. Discuss the meaning of physical features in class. Make a list of examples on the board.
2. Read the information given on "Physical Features of the Southeast" activity sheets and hold a class discussion. Include in the discussion a quick review of the vocabulary words.
3. Assign the questions in Part I as a review of the material just discussed. This may be done individually or in small groups. Review the answers for accuracy.
4. Assign Part II ("Atlas Activity") to be completed individually. Students may need to use either an atlas or a map in their text to assist with this activity. Students should do all drawing with colored pencils. All labeling on a map should be done in manuscript.

North Carolina's Outer Banks

Themes of Geography: Location, Place, Human-Environment Interaction, Movement, Region

The Southeast has several interesting groups of islands along its coast. One of the most fascinating groups is the Outer Banks of North Carolina. These barrier islands are separated from the mainland by a series of sounds. The islands jut out into the Atlantic, creating three capes. These islands are full of history and legends. From the first English colony in the New World to the daring deeds of Blackbeard the Pirate to the first flight of the Wright Brothers, there are many stories and mysteries to explore. This activity will introduce students to the Outer Banks. It will also involve them in exploring some of the interesting events that have occurred there.

Objectives
Students will
1. define geographic terms related to the Outer Banks of North Carolina.
2. research and prepare a report on one of the sites or people that has played a part in the history of the Outer Banks.
3. create a clay model of the Outer Banks, correctly labeling various points of interest.

Materials: "North Carolina's Outer Banks" activity sheets, reference books, atlases, paper, pencil, cardboard (9" x 12"), clay, toothpicks, construction paper, blue paint

Procedure

1. Introduce the terms *barrier islands, shoals,* and *reefs.* After defining the words, discuss how they would affect the coast of a state. Use as an example the Outer Banks of North Carolina.
2. Read the "North Carolina's Outer Banks" activity sheets. Discuss the material, asking students to point out interesting facts that they might enjoy learning more about. Make a list of these on the board or on chart paper. Discuss the difference between legends and historical facts. Find examples of both in the activity sheets.
3. Assign the four questions under "Student Activities." After the words are defined, discuss them in class to be certain that the meanings are clear.
4. Students should then complete activity 1 in Part II. Refer to the list of interesting facts the class has compiled. Students are to choose a topic and conduct research. They should then prepare a report to give to the entire class on their topic.
5. In the second activity, students may work in small groups or they may make individual maps. Each group will work through the following directions:
   a. Paint a piece of cardboard (9" x 12") blue to represent the Atlantic Ocean.
   b. Use clay to form an outline of the eastern coast of North Carolina and the barrier islands located off the coast.
   c. Locate each of the sites listed in activity 2 on your map.
   d. Label each site by cutting a small triangle from the construction paper. Write the name of one of the sites on the triangle. Paste the triangle on the toothpick like a flag. Put the toothpick in the clay at the appropriate spot.

Living in the Southeast

Themes of Geography: Location, Place, Human-Environment Interaction, Movement, Region

For many years, the Southeast was dependent upon only one major crop. Today the region is growing and developing a diversified economy. The majority of the people have moved from rural to urban settings; however, agriculture is still important in the region. The long growing season makes it possible to grow a variety of crops. Natural resources were one of the reasons people began to come to the area. Manufacturing plants were built close to the resources needed to produce goods. As the plants grew, more and more people were drawn to work in them. This led to the growth of cities and towns across the region. In recent years, both American and foreign companies have been attracted to the Southeast to build their plants. Many urban areas throughout the region are benefiting from this investment. This activity will provide students with a look at some of the features that are helping to provide a better way of life for people in the Southeast.

Objectives

Students will

1. identify the elements that make up the diversified economy of the Southeast today.
2. role-play selecting a site for a manufacturing plant moving into the Southeast.
3. list factors that are considered in selecting a manufacturing site.

Materials: "Living in the Southeast" activity sheets, paper, pencils, chart paper

Procedure

1. Introduce the terms *monoculture* and *diversified agriculture*. Discuss the advantages of diversified agriculture over monoculture.
2. Read the "Living in the Southeast" activity sheets. List on chart paper natural resources that have helped to attract industry to the Southeast. Ask students to explain how the development of industry has affected the lives of people in the region.
3. Students should answer the questions in Part I as a review of the printed material. Discuss the answers to make certain the responses are correct.
4. Students should work in small groups in the role-play situations. Ask them to write on chart paper the site chosen for their industry and then list the reasons for the selection. Each group should then share its results with the class.

Climate in the Southeast

Themes of Geography: Location, Place, Human-Environment Interaction, Movement, Region

The climate of a region plays an important part in the culture of the area. In the Southeast, the mild climate provides a long frost-free season for crops. The climate also affects the types of houses that are built and the clothing that is worn. More flat roofs are seen in the Southeast, where there is less snow. Lightweight clothing is usually sufficient in this region, unlike in the northern areas of the country. While there is less snow in the region, there are violent storms, such as hurricanes. These storms may move inland with winds of up to 125 miles (200 km) per hour. Entire cities are often forced to evacuate as a storm approaches. In recent years, many storms have done severe damage throughout the coastal areas of the region. This activity will show how the climate affects life in the Southeast.

Objectives

Students will

1. identify important characteristics of the climate in the Southeast.
2. use the information given on charts to explain the relationship first between latitude and the temperature and then between elevation and the temperature.

Materials: "Climate in the Southeast" activity sheets, paper, pencil, chart paper, markers

Procedure

1. Discuss how the climate of a region affects the lives of the people. Make a list of the ways on chart paper.
2. Read the "Climate in the Southeast" activity sheets. List on another sheet of chart paper characteristics of the climate in the Southeast.
3. Ask students to answer the questions in Part I of the "Student Activities" as a review of the material read. Go over the answers with the class to check for accuracy.
4. Students should work on Part II of the "Student Activities" individually. In each case, they are to read the chart and use it to answer the questions below.
5. Call on individual students to share answers as the class discusses the charts.

Urban Areas of the Southeast

Themes of Geography: Location, Place, Human-Environment Interaction, Movement, Region

The Southeast is experiencing growth. This is being reflected in the urban areas of the region. This activity will look at the five largest urban areas of this region. Students will examine some of the characteristics that have made the cities grow in recent years. They will also explain how these cities have helped the entire region to grow and develop.

Objectives

Students will

1. identify the five largest urban areas of the Southeast, based on descriptive characteristics.
2. use information in a chart to compare cities.
3. conduct research on one major city and prepare a report.
4. work with a time line to show major historic events that occurred when the largest urban areas were founded.

Materials: "Urban Areas of the Southeast" activity sheets, pencils, reference books, chart paper, 18" x 12" drawing paper

Procedure

1. Introduce the term *urban areas* and review the term *metropolitan areas.* Discuss in class characteristics of urban life as compared to rural life.
2. Read "Urban Areas of the Southeast" activity sheets. Ask students to note the characteristics of each of the five cities discussed. List these characteristics on chart paper.
3. Students should complete the activity under Part I by writing the name of the city in the blank beside the identifying characteristics. Refer to the lists on the chart paper for references.

4. Under Part II, students should write a definition of *metropolitan area* before beginning the activities. Check the definitions for accuracy.

5. Ask the class to use the information given in the chart to rank the five cities first by city population and second by metropolitan area population. Check to make certain students understand why the two figures are different.

6. In the third activity, each student should choose one of the cities and prepare a travel brochure about it. Information about the history of the city and points of interest should be included.

7. Each student should use a 18" x 12" sheet of drawing paper to design a time line. The time line should give the founding dates for each of the five cities and other historical events that happened during that time period.

Conclusion

The Southeast forms a diverse region that is ever changing. Areas of economic growth are scattered across the region. The area provides a good example of human-environment interaction, as the natural resources have been used to help bring about much of this growth. Unfortunately, in some areas the resources are becoming limited. Challenges such as these must be overcome in the future if the region is to continue to develop and progress.

Location in the Southeast

Complete each of the following activities.

1. Label each of the state capitals on the map above by placing the city and state beside the correct letter below.

A. _____   F. _____

B. _____   G. _____

C. _____   H. _____

D. _____   I. _____

E. _____   J. _____

2. Using an atlas, give the degrees of latitude and longitude for each of the following cities in the Southeast.

	Latitude	Longitude
Charleston, West Virginia	_____	_____
Mobile, Alabama	_____	_____
Birmingham, Alabama	_____	_____
Vicksburg, Mississippi	_____	_____
Jacksonville, Florida	_____	_____
Wilmington, North Carolina	_____	_____

3. Listed below are the latitude and longitude of selected cities in the Southeast. Write the names of the cities and their states in the blanks.

	Latitude	Longitude
_____	35° 7' N	90° W
_____	38° 15' N	85° 45' W
_____	38° 20' N	82° 30' W
_____	32° 4' N	81° 4' W
_____	34° 15' N	88° 42' W
_____	34° 54' N	82° 24' W

4. Read each of the relative location clues below and then identify the site by writing the answer in the blank.

a. This large lake is located in south central Florida. It is located northwest of Miami and northeast of Fort Myers. The name of the lake is _____.

b. This river forms the border between Georgia and South Carolina. The river flows southward into the Atlantic Ocean. The river is named _____.

c. This state is bordered by the Mississippi River on the west, Kentucky and Virginia on the north, North Carolina on the east, and Alabama and Georgia on the south. The state is named _____.

d. This state is bordered on the south by Florida and the Gulf of Mexico, on the east by Georgia, on the north by Tennessee, and on the west by Mississippi. The name of the state is _____.

e. This river forms the western border of West Virginia and the northern border of Kentucky. It flows into the Mississippi River. The name of the river is_____.

f. This mountain is the highest mountain east of the Mississippi River. It is located northeast of Asheville, North Carolina, in the Blue Ridge Mountains. The mountain is named _____.

g. This state is bordered on the north by North Carolina, on the west by Georgia, and on the east by the Atlantic Ocean. The state is _____.

Physical Features of the Southeast

The Southeast has ten states—Virginia, West Virginia, Kentucky, Tennessee, North Carolina, South Carolina, Georgia, Florida, Alabama, and Mississippi. Much of the Southeast is covered by coastal plains. The Atlantic Coastal Plain stretches south through Virginia, North Carolina, South Carolina, Georgia, and Florida. The Gulf Coastal Plain extends westward from Florida into Alabama and Mississippi. Both coastal plains sometimes reach as far as 200 miles (320 km) inland.

Along both coastal plains are swamps and tidewater areas. *Tidewater* is a low-lying coastal area that is often flooded by seawater. It is often hard to tell where the sea ends and the land begins when flooding is occurring. *Swamps* are low-lying areas that are always under water.

The Atlantic Coastal Plain gently rises to the Piedmont. The *Piedmont* is the upland area that lies between the coastal plain and the mountains. The fall line is located at the eastern end of the Piedmont. The *fall line* marks the point where waterfalls first appear on the rivers flowing toward the coast. This line traditionally marked the easternmost point of navigation for boats coming up the rivers from the ocean. The falls were often sources of power for factories.

To the west of the Piedmont are the Appalachian Highlands. These mountains cover a large part of the Southeast. The Blue Ridge Mountains form the easternmost range of the Appalachians. They stretch from Pennsylvania to Georgia. These mountains contain Mount Mitchell in North Carolina, the highest peak east of the Mississippi River. Mount Mitchell rises 6,684 feet (2,037 meters).

The Allegheny Plateau is located west of the Blue Ridge. The Cumberland Mountains are south of this rugged plateau. The Cumberland Mountains are really part of the Cumberland Plateau. This plateau stretches from West Virginia south through Kentucky, Virginia, Tennessee, and Alabama. The Great Smoky Mountains stretch into southwestern North Carolina, Tennessee, and Alabama.

Traveling further west, the mountains and plateaus give way to rolling hills. This region in central Kentucky and Tennessee is actually part of the Interior Plains. Finally, the hills give way to lowlands. These lowlands are part of the Ohio and Mississippi River valleys.

Rivers and streams are important to the Southeast. The Mississippi River forms the western border of Tennessee and most of Mississippi. The Ohio River forms the borders of West Virginia and Kentucky. The Cumberland River begins in Kentucky and loops down into Tennessee before flowing back through Kentucky to join the Ohio. The Tennessee River is very important to the Southeast. At one time it flooded nearby land nearly every year. But in 1933, Congress set up the Tennessee Valley Authority (TVA). Dams were built on the river to control flooding. The dams also provided water for irrigation and power generation. The TVA also introduced soil conservation methods to people living in the area. The Tennessee River has also been made navigable from Knoxville, Tennessee, to where it joins the Ohio River in Kentucky.

Student Activities

Part I. Answer the following questions about the Southeast.

1. Much of the Southeast region of the United States is covered by two coastal plains called_____and _____.

2. The Atlantic Coastal Plain runs through the following states: _____ _____

3. The Gulf Coastal Plain runs through the following states: _____ _____

4. What is a tidewater area? _____

5. What is the difference between a tidewater area and a swamp? _____ _____

6. The region that is the upland area between the coastal plain and the mountains is called the _____.

7. The highest mountain peak east of the Mississippi River is _____, located in the state of _____.

8. The Appalachian Highlands contain several major mountain ranges including the _____, _____, and _____.

9. The central regions of Kentucky and Tennessee are actually part of the _____ _____.

10. Four major rivers that flow through the Southeast are the _____, _____, _____, and _____.

11. Describe what the Tennessee Valley Authority (TVA) has been able to do to help the Southeast. _____ _____ _____ _____

Atlas Activity

Part II

1. Use an atlas or other reference books to complete the map above by labeling the following areas.

   a. Atlantic Coastal Plains   e. Mount Mitchell

   b. Gulf Coastal Plains   f. Cumberland Mountains

   c Piedmont   g. Great Smoky Mountains

   d. Blue Ridge Mountains   h. Interior Plains

2. Use a blue colored pencil to draw the following rivers on the map.

   a. Mississippi River   c. Ohio River

   b. Cumberland River   d. Tennessee River

North Carolina's Outer Banks

The Southeast contains several groups of interesting islands. One such group is found along the coast of North Carolina. The Outer Banks is the name of a line of *barrier islands.* A barrier island is a long, narrow, sandy island separated from the mainland by a lagoon.

The banks once formed a part of a major disaster area for sailing ships. There have been hundreds of shipwrecks along the Outer Banks. In fact, the area has been nicknamed the Graveyard of the Atlantic. The water is shallow in this area and there are *shoals* and *reefs.* Shoals are underwater sandbars. The water above these sandbars is very shallow. Reefs are chains of rocks at or near the surface of the water.

The Outer Banks jut out into the ocean, forming Cape Hatteras, Cape Lookout, and Cape Fear. They also form the eastern border of the Albemarle, Currituck, and Pamlico Sounds. Two large sections of the Outer Banks are taken up by the Cape Hatteras National Seashore and the Cape Lookout National Seashore. State Highway 12 provides the only transportation link across the islands which stretch for over 100 miles along the coast.

Many historic sites are located on the Outer Banks. At Corolla, near the Virginia border, the Currituck Beach Lighthouse has been warning ships of danger since 1875. Near the lighthouse is a group of wild ponies. Legends say that the ponies here and on Ocracoke Island are descendants of horses that survived shipwrecks off the coast of North Carolina.

The Wright Brothers National Memorial stands in the village of Kill Devil Hills. Orville and Wilbur Wright invented and built the first successful airplane. Here on December 17, 1903, the first power-driven, heavier-than-air machine flight occurred in the United States. With Orville at the controls, the plane flew 120 feet (37 meters) and was in the air for 12 seconds. This site was chosen because of the soft sandy surface for a landing and the strong wind that is usually blowing.

Just south of Kill Devil Hills is Jockey's Ridge State Park, which houses the highest sand dunes on the east coast. Nearby is the village of Nags Head. Legends say the name came from pirates tying a lantern around the head of a nag (mule) and letting the animal walk across the sand dunes. Ships would see the light and mistake it for a lighthouse. When they sailed to the shore, the reefs and shoals would sink their ships and allow the pirates to collect the goods.

Roanoke Island is the site of the first attempt by the English to colonize the New World. The north end of the 12-mile-long island is the site of Fort Raleigh, where the English established a colony in 1585. The colony was forced to return to England in 1586, but a second group of more than 100 colonists returned to the island in 1587. Virginia Dare became the first child of English parents to be born in America. Ships which had been sent back to England for supplies were delayed for three years because of a war with Spain. When the ships returned, there was no sign of the colonists. The fate of the "Lost Colony" continues to be a mystery today.

The Cape Hatteras Lighthouse, on Hatteras Island, is the tallest brick lighthouse on the American Coast; it is 208 feet tall. The Chicamacomico Lifesaving Station was built in 1874. It has a long history of historic rescues from the Graveyard of the Atlantic. Ocracoke Island, which is 14 miles in length, is home to Ocracoke Village, a picturesque fishing village. It was from this island that Blackbeard, the pirate, terrorized any ship that dared to come near. It was also here in 1718 that he lost his life.

Student Activities

Part I. Answer the following questions about the Outer Banks.

1. Define *barrier islands*._____

2. Define *shoals*. _____

3. Define *reefs*._____

4. Why was the name Graveyard of the Atlantic given to this region?_____

Part II. Complete the following activities.

1. Many interesting stories and legends exist about the people and locations on the Outer Banks. Choose one of the persons or sites mentioned in the article and conduct additional research to make a report for the class. Suggested topics for reports could include the following: Orville and Wilbur Wright, Sir Walter Raleigh, The Lost Colony, Blackbeard, or Cape Hatteras.

2. Research the Outer Banks in reference books and atlases. Then prepare a clay model of the Outer Banks. Use toothpicks with small labeling flags made from construction paper to mark points of interest. Be certain to include Kill Devil Hills, Nags Head, Cape Hatteras, Corolla, Hatteras Island, and Ocracoke. Other sites may be added.

Living in the Southeast

For many years, cotton was the major crop of the Southeast. However, this *monoculture,* the growing of only one crop year after year, depletes soil nutrients. Today a wide variety of crops are grown in this region. It has become a region of *diversified agriculture.* The two coastal plains produce many kinds of fruits and vegetables. Near the mouth of the Mississippi River, cotton, rice, and sugar cane are grown. The Piedmont is noted for tobacco, peaches, and dairy cattle. Corn and apples grow well in the valleys of the Appalachian Mountains. Farmers are also raising cattle, hogs, and chickens. Soybeans have become one of the most valuable crops in the Southeast.

At one time, most people in the Southeast lived on farms. However, most people now live in cities and work in factories or offices. Many industries have moved to the Southeast to be near the natural resources found there.

The forests of the Southeast provide many useful products. Southern pine is plentiful on the Coastal Plain, and hardwoods are plentiful in the Appalachians. Much of the original growth of trees has been cut, and the forest cover today is regrowth. Nearly half of the nation's commercial forests are located in the Southeast. Softwood forests help to support the paper industry. The furniture industry relies on the hardwood forests.

Major natural resources of the region include coal and phosphates. The coal-mining industry is centered near rich coal deposits in the Appalachian Mountains. One of the nation's largest bituminous (soft) coal areas is found in western Pennsylvania and West Virginia. Coal mining is still a part of the economy of Kentucky and Tennessee. Local coal and iron deposits helped to bring the steel industry to Birmingham, Alabama. The city is located near the deposits of coal, limestone, and iron that are needed to make steel. Steel production is down today because all the iron has been mined. Imported iron must be used. Phosphates, used in the manufacture of fertilizers, are mined near Tampa, Florida, and in North Carolina and Tennessee.

Name _____

The Southeast now contains nearly 90 percent of the American textile industry. The industry is heavily concentrated in the Piedmont regions of Georgia, South Carolina, North Carolina, and Virginia. The largest cotton and synthetic fiber mills are located near cities such as Asheville and Charlotte, North Carolina, and Roanoke, Virginia.

Many new manufacturing plants are opening across the Southeast. Both American and foreign companies are being attracted to the area because of lower labor costs, good port and airport access, less expensive land, and warm climate. Cities such as Tampa and Orlando, Florida; Raleigh, North Carolina; and Nashville, Tennessee are benefiting from these new industries and research facilities.

Student Activities

Part I. Answer each of the following questions based on the selection you just read.

1. Explain the difference between *monoculture* and *diversified agriculture*.

   _____

   _____

2. What two industries are dependent on the forests of the Southeast?

   _____

3. What natural resources helped to build the steel industry in Birmingham, Alabama?

   _____

   Give at least one reason for the decreased production of steel in Birmingham today.

   _____

4. Phosphates are used in the manufacturing of _____.

   Give three locations where phosphates are mined. _____

   _____, _____

5. Where is the textile industry most heavily located? _____

   _____

6. What features are attracting both American and foreign industries to the Southeast?

   _____

Part II. Complete the following activity.

Role-play the following situation. You are a member of a committee that is looking for a site to build a new manufacturing plant in the Southeast. It is vital to your company that you have access to good transportation. Work in a small group to decide what type of manufacturing plant you will build. Then, refer to an atlas or state map to decide on a location for your factory. Prepare a list of reasons why you have decided to build at that location. What preparations would you need to make to help your factory be successful? Make a list of these preparations. Share your ideas with the rest of the class.

Climate in the Southeast

For parts of the Southeast, the average temperature rarely gets below 60° F (16° C) even in January. In other areas, the average temperature in January is 32° F (0° C). Generally, the warmer temperatures are found in the southern coastal plains and in the lowlands west of the mountains. In these areas the *frost-free season* may last for six months or more. The frost-free season is the period when the temperature is always above freezing. This provides a long growing season for most of the region.

The coolest parts of the Southeast are the hills and mountains. *Elevation* is one of the main reasons for temperature differences in the Southeast. However, this is not the only reason. Otherwise Norfolk, Virginia, and Miami, Florida, would have the same climate. They are both on the Atlantic Coastal Plain and have an elevation of less than 30 feet (9 meters). Norfolk has a yearly average temperature of 59° F (15° C), while Miami has a yearly average of 76° F (24° C). The difference is their latitude. Miami is closer than Norfolk to the equator. Miami is located at 26° N, while Norfolk is at 37° N.

The precipitation in the Southeast is mostly rain. Snow is rare, except in the mountains and the northern areas of the region. Rainfall varies from about 40 inches (100 cm) a year to almost 70 inches (180 cm). The largest rainfalls are along the coasts. Since most of the rain falls during the summer when the temperature is at its highest, this combination produces hot, *humid* summers. A humid climate is one that is damp or wet.

The coastal states do not get much snow, but they do get storms. *Hurricanes* often pass through the area. A hurricane is a tropical storm with strong winds and heavy rains. The storm has spinning walls of moist air around an inner area or *eye.* The storm may be from 100 to 300 miles (160 to 480 km) wide. The winds of a hurricane may range from 75 to 125 miles (120 to 200 km) an hour. The storms that hit the Southeast usually form over the Atlantic Ocean east of the Caribbean. Storms move west and northwest into the Caribbean and the Gulf of Mexico, hitting the land in their paths. Some storms change their westward movement and head north and northeast. These storms may hit the eastern Atlantic coast.

Name _____

Student Activities

Part I. Answer the following questions about the weather in the Southeast.

1. What is the frost-free season? _____

2. What are the coolest parts of the Southeast region? _____

3. Name the two factors that play an important part in determining the average temperature of areas in the Southeast. _____ and _____

4. What is a hurricane? _____

5. What is a humid climate? _____

Part II. Study the following charts and complete the activities.

The Effect of Latitude on Temperature

City	Latitude	Average Yearly Temperature
Norfolk, Virginia	37° N	59° F (15° C)
Wilmington, North Carolina	34° N	64° F (18° C)
Savannah, Georgia	32° N	66° F (19° C)
Tampa, Florida	28° N	72° F (22° C)
Miami, Florida	26° N	76° F (24° C)

1. Which of the cities above is the farthest from the equator? _____

2. Which of the cities above is the closest to the equator? _____

3. What happens to the temperature as you move closer to the equator? _____

_____

4. What causes this to happen? _____

_____

The Effect of Elevation on Temperature

City	Latitude	Average Yearly Temperature
Charleston, South Carolina	40 ft. (12 m)	65° F (18° C)
Atlanta, Georgia	1,010 ft. (308 m)	61° F (16° C)
Raleigh, North Carolina	434 ft. (132 m)	59° F (15° C)
Asheville, North Carolina	2,140 ft. (652 m)	56° F (13° C)
Richmond, Virginia	164 ft. (50 m)	58° F (14° C)
Beckley, West Virginia	2,504 ft. (763 m)	51° F (11° C)

5. The pairs of cities in the chart above are grouped by their latitude. However, the elevation of each city varies. What is the effect of elevation on the temperature?

_____

_____

Urban Areas of the Southeast

Major cities in the Southeast are experiencing rapid growth. The study of urban geography will show some of the reasons for this growth and development. The five largest cities in the Southeast are Jacksonville, Florida; Memphis, Tennessee; Nashville, Tennessee; Charlotte, North Carolina; and Atlanta, Georgia.

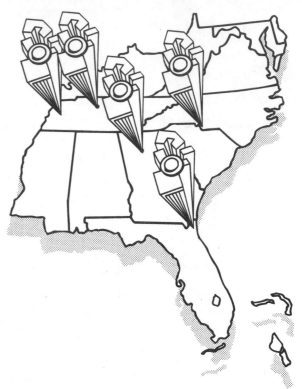

Jacksonville is the largest city in Florida as well as the state's financial and insurance capital. It is also an important seaport and a major distribution and transportation center for the southeastern United States. The city lies in the northeastern part of Florida, midway between Atlanta and Miami. Located on the St. Johns River, Jacksonville is one of Florida's busiest ports. Shipbuilding and ship repair are also important industries.

Jacksonville has about 700 factories that employ about 30,000 people. The chief industry is food processing. Other important industries include printing and publishing, chemical manufacturing, paper and pulp products, and plastics. Jacksonville is also a major banking center and home to about 35 insurance companies.

Located on a bluff on the east bank of the Mississippi River, Memphis, Tennessee, is in the southwest corner of the state. Memphis serves as the commercial and industrial center for western Tennessee and parts of neighboring states. The downtown area of Memphis extends one and one half miles (2.4 kilometers) along the Mississippi River. The city has become a center for higher education, medical care, motel development, and the recording and distribution of music.

Memphis has one of the busiest inland ports on the Mississippi River, handling more than 13 million short tons of freight yearly. The port ships goods to all parts of the world. Memphis is also the headquarters of Federal Express, the nation's largest overnight air express delivery service. The major manufacturing companies in Memphis produce chemicals, electrical equipment, food and food products, and paper and related products.

Nashville is the state capital of Tennessee. It is sometimes called Music City, U.S.A., because it is a recording and broadcasting center for country music. More than 180 recording companies, 23 recording studios, and about 450 song-publishing firms operate in the city. In addition, the production of printed materials is among the city's most important industries. Other major products include aircraft parts, food products, glass, heating and cooking equipment, tires, and trucks. The city is situated on a bluff overlooking the west bank of the Cumberland River.

Charlotte, North Carolina, lies about 15 miles north of the North Carolina-South Carolina border. It is in the southern half of the Piedmont region. The southern Piedmont leads the United States in textile production. Charlotte provides banking, insurance, wholesaling, and medical services for this region. The textile industry has helped Charlotte to become one of the nation's chief trucking centers.

Atlanta is the capital of Georgia. It is a center for trade and transportation for the southeastern United States. Atlanta lies in northern Georgia, in the foothills of the Blue Ridge Mountains. The city has been a railroad center since the 1840s. A web of railroads branching from its strategic location makes it a distribution center as well as a commercial, financial, and industrial giant.

The city has had several periods of industrial expansion and construction growth. Today, it is the center of one of the fastest-growing U.S. urban areas. The Atlanta metropolitan area is a center for service industries. It ranks as a leader in wholesale and retail trade, transportation, and communication. The chief manufactured products of the Atlanta area include food, transportation equipment, tobacco products, electronics, and textiles. The Coca-Cola Company has its headquarters in Atlanta and has some manufacturing in the city.

Student Activities

Part I. Complete the following activity by matching the name of the city with its description. The names may be used more than once.

Jacksonville   Memphis   Charlotte   Atlanta   Nashville

_____   1. Located in the foothills of the Blue Ridge Mountains, the city has been a railroad center since the 1840s.

_____   2. Often called Music City, U.S.A., this city is home to over 180 recording companies, 23 recording studios, and about 450 song-publishing companies.

_____   3. This busy inland port on the Mississippi River ships goods to all parts of the world.

_____   4. This city is located in the southern Piedmont, which leads the United States in textile production.

_____   5. This port city is located halfway between Atlanta and Miami.

_____ 6. In addition to being the headquarters of Federal Express, this city is a center for the recording and distribution of music.

_____ 7. A major banking and insurance center, this city also has important printing and publishing industries, chemical manufacturing, paper and pulp products, and plastics.

_____ 8. The textile industry helped to make this city one of the United States' chief trucking centers.

_____ 9. This state capital is also the home to Coca-Cola.

_____ 10. Located on a bluff overlooking the Cumberland River, this city has the production of printed materials as one of its most important industries.

Part II. Use the chart below to complete these activities.

City	Population (1990)	Rank	Date Founded	Metropolitan Area Population
Atlanta	393,929	36	1837	2,959,950
Charlotte	395,925	35	1748	1,162,093
Jacksonville	672,971	15	1822	906,727
Memphis	610,337	18	1819	1,007,306
Nashville	510,784	23	1779	985,026

1. Research and explain the meaning of a metropolitan area._____

_____

2. List these five cities in size (largest to smallest) according to city population and then according to metropolitan area population.

City Population   Metropolitan Area

_____   _____

_____   _____

_____   _____

_____   _____

_____   _____

3. Choose one of the cities in the chart above; research and prepare a report about it. Include information about the founding of the city and its major points of interest. Prepare a travel brochure for the city. Share your brochure with the class.

4. Prepare a time line showing the dates of the founding of these cities. Research to find important historical events that happened near these dates that could be added to the time line.

The North Central States

│

Goals for This Unit

Students will

1. use atlases to find the absolute and relative location of sites in the North Central States.
2. create a travel brochure to attract tourists to regions of the North Central States.
3. identify and label the key physical features of the North Central States.
4. use the city of Chicago as a study of human-environment interaction and the development of regions.
5. identify and locate the three major agricultural belts located in the North Central States.
6. discuss the economic importance of the Great Lakes to the North Central States.
7. list factors that are important to the development of industries within a region.

Rationale

The North Central States are often referred to as the "Breadbasket of America" because of the amount of wheat that is grown in the region. However, the region has much more to offer than wheat fields. Both the Corn Belt and Wheat Belt are found in these states. In addition to agricultural products, the region is a large industrial center. The Great Lakes have provided a source of cheap transportation for both raw materials and manufactured goods. The study of this region demonstrates people's ability to interact with natural surroundings to improve their style of living. The locks and canals connecting the Great Lakes and the St. Lawrence River now provide access to the Atlantic Ocean for ports that are 1,000 miles (1,800 km) inland. These changes have had a dramatic effect on the progress in the region.

Skills Taught in This Unit		
using atlases	using latitude and longitude grids	
reading and labeling maps	interpreting charts	
collecting data	role-playing	

Vocabulary

glaciers	badlands	bluffs
canals	locks	St. Lawrence Seaway
Soo Canals	Welland Ship Canal	corn-fed livestock
crop rotation	shelterbelts	

Background Information

The North Central States region stretches for nearly 1,000 miles (1,800 km) from east to west and about 800 miles (1,300 km) from north to south. The region is bordered by the Great Lakes and Canada to the north. It is a region that has important agricultural areas as well as major industrial centers. It is a very diverse region economically and ethnically. Many immigrants have moved to make their homes in this region. This has added to the development and multicultural flavor of the area.

Location in the North Central States

Themes of Geography: Location, Region

The North Central States get their name from being located in the central part of the United States next to Canada and the Great Lakes. These states are between the Middle Atlantic States to the east and the Rocky Mountain States to the west. Major transportation routes serve to connect the area with the entire United States. This activity will help students to understand both the absolute and relative location of this area. Students will work with an atlas and other reference books to help find the answers to questions dealing with location.

Objectives

Students will
1. use an atlas to identify specific political and physical regions of the North Central States.
2. identify major cities and capitals by writing the names of the states in which they are located and labeling them on a map.
3. use clues of latitude and longitude coordinates to identify selected North Central States.

Materials: "Location in the North Central States" student activity sheets, classroom atlases, pencils, textbooks, reference books

Procedure

1. Introduce the North Central States to the class. Find the states on a map and discuss their location. Review with the class both relative and absolute location.
2. Read aloud the introductory paragraphs of "Location in the North Central States" student activity sheets.
3. Ask students to use an atlas or other reference books to answer the first three questions.
4. Students should write the state beside each city in question 4 and then write the name of the city beside the appropriate symbol on the map.
5. Using atlases, students should locate the state represented by each set of absolute location coordinates.
6. Go over the answers to all questions in class to check for understanding.

Physical Features of the North Central States

Most of the area covered by the North Central States lies within the rolling Interior Plains of the United States. Only the hills of the Canadian Shield around the northern Great Lakes and the Ozarks in southern Missouri are in other landform regions. However, there are several interesting physical features that lie within these states. The thousands of lakes in the northern section were carved out by glaciers. The Badlands found in the Dakotas and Nebraska are mainly the result of erosion by water. The Black Hills of South Dakota rose from pressure beneath the earth's surface that caused the crust to rise and form a huge dome. The Ozark Plateau is a region dominated by forested hills and low mountains. In addition, three major river systems play an important part in the life of this region. This activity will focus on these special features of the North Central States.

Objectives

Students will
1. identify and locate on a map the major physical features of the North Central States.
2. design a travel brochure to attract tourists to one of the regions of these states.
3. identify and label the 12 political regions making up the North Central States.

Materials: "Physical Features of the North Central States" student activity sheets, colored pencils, pencils, atlases, reference books, drawing paper

Procedure

1. Read "Physical Features of the North Central States" student activity sheets.
2. Discuss the physical features in class and make a list of major features found in the North Central States.
3. Students should answer questions 1–8 in Part I as a review of the material read.
4. Students will use atlases or reference books to draw and label on the map the physical features listed under the first activity in Part II.
5. Students will label the 12 states in the region in activity #2.
6. Remind students to use colored pencils when coloring the map in activity 3.
7. Students should use drawing paper and colored pencils or crayons to complete the brochure for activity 4. Remind students that most brochures are tri-folds. Completed brochures should be displayed in the room or hallway.

Chicago

Chicago is the largest city in the North Central States. It is located at the southern end of Lake Michigan. It is also connected by rivers to the Mississippi River, making it a major trade and transportation center. Chicago is the busiest port on the Great Lakes and is home to the busiest airport in the world. The Chicago River is a study in human-environment interaction. Engineers have actually reversed the flow of the river to avoid dumping more pollution into Lake Michigan. The city also provides a study of diverse regions. Each section of Chicago has characteristics that are uniquely its own. This activity will examine the regions of Chicago and focus on how the people have helped each to develop in a separate way.

Materials: "Chicago" student activity sheets, reference books, travel guides, hotel directories, calculators

Procedure
1. Read "Chicago" student activity sheets in class.
2. List on the board each region of Chicago and the characteristics that make that region unique.
3. Discuss the theme of Human-Environment Interaction. Ask students to identify examples of this theme that are mentioned in the activity sheets. These examples should also be listed on the board.
4. As a review, ask the class to answer questions 1–6 under Part I. Go over the answers in class.
5. Students will need to read the chart and complete the required calculations in activity 1 of Part II. Calculators may be used for this activity.
6. Divide students into small groups to begin work on planning a trip to Chicago. Remind the groups that they must keep a budget and make a detailed report of the cost of the trip. Information found in motel/hotel directories, reference books, and travel guides should be used in the activity. The final report should include the following parts: recommended length and dates of travel, travel arrangements, lodging, sites to visit, and the budget.

The Great Lakes

The Great Lakes, located between the United States and Canada, are the world's largest group of freshwater lakes. These lakes were formed millions of years ago by glaciers that scraped out the depressions and then melted to gradually fill them with water. Today the Great Lakes are connected by a series of locks and canals to the St.

Lawrence River. This system allows cities that are as far inland as 1,000 miles (1,600 kilometers) to ship goods around the world. The lakes have provided a cheap means of transportation for goods among the states and provinces surrounding them and with the rest of the world. This activity will look at the Great Lakes and the movement of goods that takes place each day. Students will also realize that the locks and canals are examples of human-environment interaction.

Objectives
Students will
1. identify and label the Great Lakes and the major port cities on the lakes.
2. explain how the locks and canals have helped the growth and economy of the North Central States.
3. read a novel relating to the Great Lakes and the St. Lawrence Seaway.
4. role-play a situation (described on the student page) and write a story of the events that occurred.

Materials: "The Great Lakes" student activity sheets, paper, pencils, copies of *Paddle to the Sea* by Holling C. Holling, atlases, reference books

Procedure
1. Read in class "The Great Lakes" student activity sheets.
2. Discuss the ways the Great Lakes have affected the lives of the people in the North Central States.
3. List ways that people have changed their environment to make the lakes even more beneficial.
4. Students should answer questions 1–10 under Part I as a review. Go over the answers in class.
5. In activity #1 under Part II, students should write the state on the line beside each port city and then write the name of the city beside the appropriate symbol on the map.
6. *Paddle to the Sea* is the story of a small wooden boat that floats through the Great Lakes to the St. Lawrence River and eventually comes to the Atlantic Ocean. If there are several copies of the book available, assign it to be read by students. If only one copy is available, read it in the classroom.
7. After reading *Paddle to the Sea*, students should be able to role-play taking such a trip and write a creative story about their adventures.

Agricultural Regions of the North Central States

The North Central States are often referred to as the "Breadbasket of the United States." There are actually three distinct agricultural regions or belts in this area. They include the Corn Belt, the Wheat Belt, and the Dairy Belt. Each belt is located in a separate part of the region and is vital to the economic well-being of the region. This activity will look at each of these belts. Characteristics of each belt will be noted along with agricultural practices that are used to help produce the crops each year.

Objective

Students will

1. identify the major agricultural crops and their location within the North Central States.
2. create a bulletin board map showing the crops and develop a key to explain the map.
3. discuss methods of soil conservation, such as crop rotation.

Materials: "Agricultural Regions of the North Central States" student activity sheets, paper, pencils, watercolor markers, reference books, atlases

Procedure

1. Read "Agricultural Regions of the North Central States" student activity sheets in class.
2. Discuss the important role of agriculture in the economic development of the North Central States.
3. Ask students to identify and explain agricultural practices that have been developed by farmers to protect the soil of the area.
4. Students should answer questions 1–6 under Part I as a review of the lesson. Go over the answers in class.
5. The activity in Part II should be done in small groups. Each group of four or five students will develop a map of the region and show the major agricultural products. The three major belts should be identified on the maps. A series of symbols should be included in a key to help explain the map to other students. Display the finished products in the classroom or in hallways.

Conclusion

The North Central States form a diverse region that is dependent on both agriculture and industry. The people have taken the natural resources that they found and interacted with them to establish a very efficient farming and industrial base for their way of life. The region provides clear examples of the five geographical themes and how they are a part of the daily lives of the people in this area.

Location in the North Central States

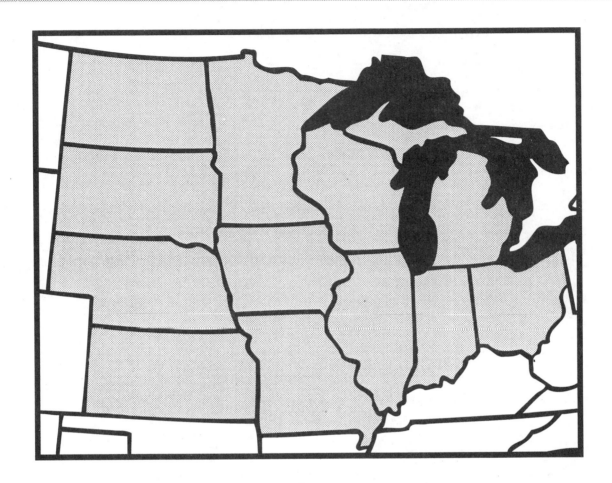

Determining Location in the North Central States

Twelve states are included in the North Central States region. These states are Ohio, Indiana, Illinois, Michigan, Wisconsin, Minnesota, Iowa, Missouri, Kansas, Nebraska, South Dakota, and North Dakota. The region is noted for farms, forests, and factories. However, farms make the region unique. This region is known as the "Breadbasket of the United States." When the Canadian Provinces of Manitoba, Alberta, and Saskatchewan are added, the extended region is often labeled "the Breadbasket of the World" because of the large amounts of wheat produced here. In addition to wheat, the states produce large amounts of corn, soybeans, vegetables, milk, and meat.

The region stretches between 36° N and 49° N latitude and 81° W and 104° W longitude. The region measures about 1,000 miles (1,800 km) from east to west and about 800 miles (1,300 km) from north to south. It borders three Canadian Provinces, four of the Great Lakes, and nine states.

Student Activities

Use an atlas or your textbook to help locate the North Central States by identifying the following:

1. Three Canadian Provinces bordering the North Central States to the north:

   _____   _____   _____

2. Four Great Lakes bordering the North Central States:

   _____   _____   _____   _____

3. Nine states bordering the North Central States:

   _____   _____   _____

   _____   _____   _____

   _____   _____   _____

4. Listed below are major cities located in the North Central States. Identify each city by writing the name of the state in which it is located on the line. (Abbreviations may be used.) Then, label the city on the map on the preceding page.

   Chicago _____   Detroit _____   St. Paul _____
   Lansing _____   Bismarck _____   Columbus _____
   Indianapolis _____   Springfield _____   Jefferson City _____
   Pierre _____   Topeka _____   Des Moines _____
   Madison _____   Milwaukee _____   Minneapolis _____
   Lincoln _____   St. Louis _____   Cleveland _____

5. Identify these selected North Central States that are located at each of the following coordinates of latitude and longitude:

   a. Latitude 48°N
      Longitude 100°W _____

   b. Latitude 44°N
      Longitude 88°W _____

   c. Latitude 40°N
      Longitude 92°W _____

   d. Latitude 40°N
      Longitude 84°W _____

   e. Latitude 38°N
      Longitude 98°W _____

   f. Latitude 40°N
      Longitude 88° W _____

   g. Latitude 44°N
      Longitude 100°W _____

   h. Latitude 48°N
      Longitude 98°W _____

Physical Features of the North Central States

Almost the entire North Central States region lies within the rolling Interior Plains. Only the hills of the Canadian Shield around Lake Superior and the Ozarks in southern Missouri are in other landform regions.

During the last ice age, *glaciers* extended as far south as the Missouri and Ohio Rivers. A glacier is a thick mass of ice that slides slowly across the earth's surface. The northern portion of the region was glacially eroded, leaving behind scoured rocks, thin soils, and thousands of lakes. Minnesota alone has more than 10,000 lakes. The southern part of the region generally has thick, rich soils that were deposited by the glaciers.

A region of badlands is found in North and South Dakota and parts of Nebraska. *Badlands* are small, steep hills and deep gullies formed primarily by water erosion. Flash floods produce the most erosion in badland regions and commonly wear away large areas. There is little or no vegetation in the deep gullies and high steeped *bluffs* of the badlands. The bedrock of the badlands consists of thick, weakly cemented layers of rock. The soil of the badlands is composed of sand and gravel with layers of clay, limestone, and sandstone. More than 240,000 acres (97,000 hectares) has been set aside in South Dakota as the Badlands National Monument.

The Black Hills are a range of low mountains found in southwestern South Dakota and eastern Wyoming. The Black Hills cover 6,000 square miles (16,000 square kilometers). They rise from 2,000 to 4,000 feet (610 to 1,200 meters) above the surrounding plains. The Black Hills were formed millions of years ago when pressure from below raised the crust of the earth into a huge dome. Erosion wore this dome into the gigantic rock mountains that are now the Black Hills.

The Ozark Plateau is Missouri's largest land region. It is a region dominated by forested hills and low mountains. The plateau rises from 500 to 1,700 feet (150 to 518 meters) above sea level. In the extreme southwestern corner of the state, a high, wooded tableland has soil good enough for gardening and raising strawberries. The river valleys are about the only level land in the Ozark region. The plateau is noted for its many caves, large springs and lakes, and clear, fast-flowing streams.

The river channels of the North Central States were formed largely by melted ice from glaciers. The region today is drained by the upper Mississippi River system. The major tributaries of the Mississippi include such large rivers as the Ohio, Missouri, and Illinois. The Ohio River flows along the southern borders of Ohio and Indiana and the southeastern edge of Illinois. There, it reaches the Mississippi River. The Missouri River enters the North Central region in North Dakota. It flows through 6 of the 12 states in the region. Near St. Louis, Missouri, it joins the Mississippi River. The Missouri has six major dams that have been built to control flooding. The Illinois River begins about 45 miles (72 kilometers) southwest of Chicago and flows across Illinois to join the Mississippi River about 50 miles (80 kilometers) above St. Louis. The river forms the southern part of the Illinois waterway which connects Lake Michigan with the Mississippi River.

All three rivers have been dredged and channeled to allow barge traffic between the North Central States and the Gulf of Mexico. Bulk freight, such as iron ore, coal, and grain, moved on the rivers can reach nearly every major city of the North Central States and the Great Lakes.

The Mississippi River, the largest river in the United States, starts as a stream in northern Minnesota in the Lake Itasca area. As it flows south, it forms the borders of the North Central States of Wisconsin, Iowa, Illinois, and Missouri. It eventually flows into the Gulf of Mexico.

Student Activities

Part I. Answer the following questions about the physical features of the North Central States.

1. Most of the landforms in the North Central States are composed of _____.

2. What effect did the movement of glaciers have on the landforms of the northern and southern parts of the North Central States? _____

_____

3. What are *badlands*? _____

_____

    In what states are badlands found? _____

4. What caused the Black Hills to rise up in South Dakota and Wyoming? _____

_____

_____

5. What is the name of Missouri's largest land region? _____

6. What physical features are found in the Ozark Plateau? _____

_____

7. What major river system drains the North Central States? _____

8. Name three major rivers that feed into this system._____

_____

Part II. Complete each of the following activities.

1. Listed below are major physical features found in the North Central States. Label them on the map above, printing their names in the appropriate locations.

Land Features	**Rivers and Lakes**
Black Hills	Missouri River
Ozark Plateau	Illinois River
Badlands	Ohio River
	Mississippi River
	Lake Itasca

2. Label the 12 political regions found in the North Central region. Print the name of each North Central State on the map in its proper location.

3. Color the map. All of the North Central States should be colored a light yellow. All rivers and lakes should be outlined and colored blue. All surrounding land should be colored light brown.

4. Role-play that you have been selected to design a brochure to attract tourists to one of the regions within the North Central States. Decide which region you will represent. Then, make a brochure that will urge tourists to come to your region.

Chicago

Chicago is the third largest city in the United States. It stretches along 25 miles (40 kilometers) of the southwest shore of Lake Michigan. It covers 228 square miles (591 square kilometers) and lies on a plain that is 595 feet (181 meters) above sea level. About 3 million people live in Chicago. The metropolitan area is home to about 7.5 million.

Chicago was originally the site of Fort Dearborn. It became a city in 1837. Its location at the tip of Lake Michigan and its role as a major terminal for railroads caused it to grow rapidly. Today it is an important center of transportation for the United States. Chicago is the busiest port on the Great Lakes and has the world's busiest airport.

The Chicago River flows westward from Lake Michigan near the center of the city. It is known as the river that flows backwards. Until 1900, the river flowed into the lake. However, engineers reversed the flow to prevent sewage in the river from polluting the lake, which supplies the water for the city. The river was made to flow westward through the construction of the Chicago Sanitary and Ship Canal. It was the first river in the world to flow away from its mouth. About a mile from Lake Michigan, the river divides, with one branch flowing northwest and the other south. The southern branch flows into the Des Plaines River which connects with the Illinois River and eventually the Mississippi River.

Chicago has four main sections—Downtown, the North Side, the West Side, and the South Side. Downtown Chicago is noted for its skyscrapers, department stores, and Grant Park. Included among the buildings is the 110-story Sears Tower, one of the world's tallest buildings, rising to 1,454 feet (443 meters). North of the Chicago River, Michigan Avenue forms the core of the downtown area. This area has been named the Magnificent Mile because of its many elegant stores, hotels, restaurants, and office buildings.

The North Side is almost entirely residential. Nearly one million people live in this area. The North Side is a mixture of smaller areas. About 68 percent of the people in this section are white, 22 percent are Hispanic, and about 6 percent are African American. The Gold Coast is a luxurious residential area with Victorian mansions and skyscraper apartments. The Carl Sandburg Village is composed of high-rise apartment buildings. Old Town includes many gift shops, nightclubs, restaurants, and renovated old homes. Cabrini-Green is an area of public housing.

The West Side is home to about 600,000 Chicagoans. About 50 percent of the population are African American, 29 percent are Hispanic, and the rest are non-Hispanic whites. A major industrial region is located in the section. Large sections of the residential areas contain abandoned, decaying buildings. However, some community groups have begun to restore the run-down apartment buildings. The Chicago Post Office, the largest in the world, and the University of Illinois at Chicago are located in this section of the city.

The South Side is the largest section in area and population. Nearly 1.5 million people live on the South Side. This section includes industrial parks, an international port, parks, residential communities, and some poverty-stricken neighborhoods. About 60 percent of the population are African American. Other ethnic groups include people of German, Hispanic, Irish, and Polish descent. Two well-known areas in this section are Chinatown and Bridgeport. Chinatown has a small residential section, restaurants, food stores, and gift shops. Bridgeport is a community of small bungalows.

The Old Water Tower, a Chicago landmark, stands at Michigan and Chicago Avenues. The tower was one of the few structures that managed to survive the Great Chicago Fire. The summer of 1871 had been unusually dry in Chicago. On the evening of October 8, 1871, a fire started on the southwest side of town. Some historians believe it began in a barn belonging to Mrs. Patrick O'Leary, when a cow kicked over a lantern. Fanned by strong winds, the fire spread north and east through the city, consuming its many wooden buildings. The fire roared for more than 24 hours. It wiped out the downtown area and most of the North Side homes. It killed nearly 300 people and left 90,000 homeless. However, the city was rebuilt to become one of the great cities of the world.

The city of Chicago has a proud history. The flag of the city helps to tell the story. There are four red stars in a row on a white background. The first star stands for Fort Dearborn, a small military post built near the mouth of the Chicago River in 1803. From this small post, the city would grow. The second star represents the Great Chicago Fire. The other two stars represent the two world's fairs that have been held in the city. The first was the World's Columbian Exposition in 1893 to commemorate Columbus' arrival in America. The second was the Century of Progress Exposition in 1933 to celebrate the city's centennial of its incorporation as a village. The four red stars have a blue stripe above and below them to stand for the Chicago River and its two branches.

Student Activities

Part I. Answer the following questions about Chicago.

1. What are the four major sections of the city of Chicago? _____,
_____, _____, _____

2. Explain this statement: The Chicago River is a good example of human-environment interaction. _____
_____

3. What is the Magnificent Mile? _____
_____

4. What was the cause of the Great Chicago Fire? _____
What were the effects of the fire? _____
_____

5. What factors led to the early growth of the city?
_____

6. When were the two World's Fairs held in Chicago, and what was the title of each?
_____, _____

Part II. Complete each of the following activities.

1. The chart below shows the largest communities in the Chicago area. Read the chart and then answer the questions below.

Largest Communities in the Chicago Area			
Name	Population	Name	Population
Chicago	2,783,726	Arlington Heights	75,460
Aurora	99,581	Evanston	73,233
Naperville	85,351	Waukegan	69,586
Elgin	77,010	Schaumburg	68,586
Joliet	76,836	Cicero	67,438

a. What is the total population of the ten communities in the Chicago Area?
_____

b. What percent of the total population lives in the following communities?

Aurora _____   Elgin _____

Evanston _____   Cicero _____

Chicago _____   Joliet _____

2. Chicago is a city that is known for its museums and cultural events. A few of these include the Adler Planetarium featuring exhibits on the solar system and space exploration, Shedd Aquarium showing aquatic life from around the world, Field Museum with exhibits of natural history, Art Institute of Chicago containing one of the finest collections of art in the world, and Museum of Science and Industry with thousands of hands-on interactive science exhibits. Using this information and additional information found in reference books, plan a vacation to Chicago. Check hotel directories for hotels and their cost. Plan a budget that will cover all of your expenses. List the places that you would like to visit in Chicago and explain what you want to see in each place. Make a presentation to the class about your trip.

The Great Lakes

The Great Lakes are the world's largest group of freshwater lakes. They contain nearly 18 percent of the world's fresh water. Four of the lakes, Ontario, Erie, Huron, and Superior, help to form the border of Canada and the United States. Lake Michigan is completely within the United States. The lakes form the most important inland waterway in North America. They were the routes used by many of the early explorers and settlers who came to the North Central States and the province of Ontario. Later, the cheap transportation offered by the lakes helped to turn this region into one of the great industrial areas of the United States and Canada.

Over the last 2 million years, glaciers advanced south into the area of the Great Lakes. These glaciers, some of which were about 6,600 feet (2,000 meters) thick, cut out deep depressions and pushed ahead great amounts of rocks and soil. As the glaciers gradually melted, the rocks and soil that had been piled up blocked drainage. Then water gradually filled the lakes over the last 15,000 years.

Some of the ports on the Great Lakes lie over 1,000 miles (1,600 kilometers) inland, but ships can sail from these ports to any other port in the world. This is made possible by sets of *canals* and *locks* built by the governments of Canada and the United States. These canals and locks compensate for the differences in water levels of the lakes.

One major set of canals and locks is the *St. Lawrence Seaway*. The seaway extends about 450 miles (724 kilometers) from Montreal to the end of Lake Erie. Its canals and locks allow ships to sail from the Atlantic Ocean to Lake Superior. The *Welland Ship Canal* is one example of these locks and canals. Located west of the Niagara River, the locks allow ships to go around Niagara Falls.

Another set of canals and locks is called the *Soo Canals*. These canals are located on the St. Marys River, which connects Lake Superior and Lake Huron. The canals allow ships to go around the 20-foot (6-meter) drop in the St. Marys River. To reach the Atlantic, ships travel across Lake Huron, Lake Erie, Lake Ontario, and down the St. Lawrence River.

The Great Lakes and their canal and lock systems are among the busiest in the world. The Great Lakes have facilitated the industrial development of the United States and central Canada, especially in the steel industry. Iron ore is quickly carried across the lakes from Minnesota, Wisconsin, and Michigan to the steel manufacturing centers of Ontario, Indiana, Ohio, and Pennsylvania.

The Great Lakes also offer the best means of transporting the huge wheat crops from western Canada and the northern United States to milling centers in eastern Canada and in Buffalo, New York. In addition, ships carry coal, copper, flour, and manufactured goods across the lakes. The Saint Lawrence Seaway handles about 50 million short tons (45 million metric tons) of cargo annually. Most of the freight travels from Canada and the United States to countries in Europe. This freight is usually bulk cargo such as grain, minerals, and other raw materials. The seaway is the cheapest way to ship large quantities of these products. Iron ore and grain make up about 65 percent of the cargo shipped. Other freight carried on the seaway includes coal, oil, and general cargo, which consists of manufactured products, such as automobiles and steel.

Student Activities

Part I. Answer the following questions about the Great Lakes.

1. Name each of the five Great Lakes. _____ _____

   _____ _____ _____

2. Which of the Great Lakes is located entirely within the United States?

   _____

3. What percent of the world's fresh surface water supply is contained in the Great
   Lakes? _____

4. Explain how the Great Lakes were formed. _____

   _____

   _____

5. How is it possible for ships from ports over 1,000 miles (1,600 kilometers) inland
   to sail to ports around the world? _____

6. What major seaway extends about 450 miles (742 kilometers) from Montreal to
   the eastern end of Lake Erie? _____

7. How is it possible for ships to travel around Niagara Falls? _____

   _____

8. Explain how ships are able to go around the 20-foot (6-meter) drop in the St.
   Marys River between Lake Huron and Lake Erie. _____

   _____

9. Iron ore is carried from Minnesota, Wisconsin, and Michigan to steel
   manufacturing centers located in _____.

10. What are the major products shipped on the Great Lakes? _____

    _____

The Great Lakes Region

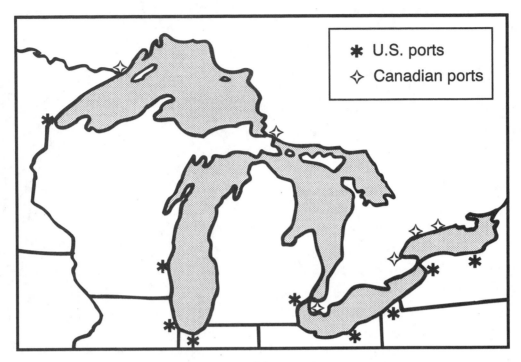

Part II. Complete each of the following activities.

1. Use an atlas or your textbook to complete this activity. Label each of the Great Lakes on the map above. Below are major cities involved in trade and transportation on the Great Lakes. Identify each city by writing its correct state or province on the line beside it. Then write the name of the city by the correct symbol on the map above.

Erie _____   Rochester _____   Buffalo _____

Gary_____   Cleveland _____   Windsor _____

Detroit_____   Chicago _____   Toronto _____

Duluth _____   Hamilton_____   Oshawa _____

Milwaukee _____   Sault St. Marie _____   Thunder Bay _____

2. Read the book *Paddle to the Sea* by Holling C. Holling. Use the map at the end of the book to trace on the map above the journey of Paddle from the cabin near Lake Nipigon through the Great Lakes to the Atlantic Ocean. Would such a trip really be possible? Why or why not? Role-play that you are on a boat on the Great Lakes. A severe storm suddenly occurs, or you find yourself being pulled to a large falls. Create a story telling what happened to you.

Agricultural Regions of the North Central States

Fertile soil, level land, hot, wet summers, and agricultural technology have helped to make the North Central States one of the leading agricultural centers in the world. This region contains three major agricultural regions—the Corn Belt, Wheat Belt, and Dairy Belt.

The Corn Belt extends generally from Ohio to eastern South Dakota. Iowa and Illinois, the leading corn-producing states, are in the center of the belt. Much of the corn raised is used to feed cattle and hogs. In fact, Iowa and Illinois are also the leading pork-producing states. Farmers here raise *corn-fed livestock*. This means that the animals are fed corn to fatten them before they are sent to market. Other uses for corn include use as food, corn oil, and corn syrup.

The Corn Belt farmers have learned that raising corn every year on the same land causes a loss of minerals in the soil. To prevent this, they either use large amounts of commercial fertilizers or they practice *crop rotation*. Crop rotation means that another crop such as soybeans or clover is substituted for corn in the fields in some years. This practice has greatly increased the amount of soybeans raised in the North Central States. Soybeans are now a major crop and an important export.

Wheat is the most important food crop in the United States. Nearly everyone eats wheat in one form or another every day. It is one of the few grains not used chiefly for animal feed. Wheat is used in breads and other baked goods and in cereals. It has become one of the nation's most important exports. The best wheat-growing areas are found west of the Corn Belt, but wheat is grown in nearly every North Central State.

The Wheat Belt includes the Spring Wheat Belt and the Winter Wheat Belt. The Spring Wheat Belt is located in eastern North Dakota and South Dakota and in western Minnesota. It is called the Spring Wheat Belt because the wheat is planted in the spring and harvested in the summer.

The Winter Wheat Belt is located farther south in eastern Nebraska and in Kansas, but it extends as far south as Texas. Winter wheat is planted in the fall and grows to a height of several inches (centimeters) before the first frost. It then remains dormant until it begins to grow again in the spring. It is harvested in the early summer.

Irrigation has allowed the growing of wheat to expand westward into the Great Plains. The amount of rainfall is very important to the wheat crops. Reduction in rainfall means either a crop failure or the necessity of using irrigation systems. Soil erosion is another concern in the Wheat Belt. In windy areas, rows of trees, called *shelterbelts*, have been planted to protect the soil. Contour plowing helps to prevent soil runoff in the more hilly and rolling fields.

The Dairy Belt, where the summers are shorter and the soils are less fertile, is located north of the Corn Belt. This region covers almost all of Wisconsin and most of Michigan and Minnesota. The region also extends into Iowa on the southwestern part of the belt and into New York and Vermont on the northeastern side. Wisconsin is often called "America's Dairyland" because it produces more milk, butter, and cheese than any other state.

Much of the land in the Dairy Belt is used for pasture and raising hay, oats, and corn to feed the cattle. Many of the farmers also grow vegetables. Some of the dairy farms also have woodlots, which can be used to provide income from firewood, maple syrup, Christmas trees, and wood pulp. Some fruit-growing areas have grown up around the Great Lakes because of the warming effect of the lakes.

Student Activities

Part I. Answer each of the following questions.

1. What are the three major agricultural belts located in the North Central States?
   _____

2. What is meant by crop rotation? _____
   _____

3. What is the most important food crop in the United States? Why?_____
   _____

4. Explain the difference between spring wheat and winter wheat. _____
   _____

5. Which state is nicknamed "America's Dairyland"?_____
   Why? _____

6. How is much of the land in the Dairy Belt used? _____
   _____

Part II. Complete the following activity.
Create a classroom bulletin board showing the major products of the North Central States. Use an overhead projector to project a map of this region onto white paper on a bulletin board. Trace the map with pencil and then watercolor markers. Cut out symbols of various agricultural products and place them on the map. Shade in the three agricultural belts studied in this lesson.

The South Central States

Goals for This Unit

Students will

1. use atlases to find the absolute and relative location of sites in the South Central States.
2. label maps locating sites and physical features in the South Central States.
3. identify the key physical characteristics of the South Central States.
4. identify problems arising from large numbers of migrations occurring at one time and suggest possible solutions.
5. identify problems arising from urbanization and suggest possible solutions.
6. identify agricultural products and explain why such a variety of crops can be produced in this region.

Rationale

The South Central States region is composed of only four states, but these states provide a wide variety of products that are important not only to the United States but to the rest of the world. The varied climate and landforms give rise to a great variety of crops and related agricultural industries. The region is also noted for its mixture of cultures. The French have made a tremendous impact on the culture of Louisiana, Spain has been a great influence in Texas, and the Native Americans have made tremendous contributions in all the states, particularly in Oklahoma. The South Central States are a study in contrasts. Yet there are many common bonds that connect the people of these states as they work to solve the problems of the future.

Skills Taught in This Unit

using atlases
reading and labeling maps
collecting data
role-playing
making graphs

using latitude and longitude grids
interpreting charts
compiling charts
making a map key
organizing materials for study

Vocabulary

gulf
feedlots
delta

brackish
levees
silt

bayous
sorghum grain

Background Information

In this study of the South Central States, students will deal with both absolute and relative location of the states and sites within the states. They will also look at the physical characteristics that help to make these states unique. The region's agriculture will be reviewed to show how the people make a living and how they have adapted their lives to their environment. The growth of cities will be studied by looking at five of the larger cities in this region. Finally, the largest one-day migration event in American history will be used to illustrate how the movement of people and ideas can cause conflict. As a result of the study, students should be able to discuss many problems that are present in this region and then propose some possible solutions.

Location in the South Central States

Themes of Geography: Location, Region

The South Central States make up a unique region of the United States. These four states are bordered by six states and one foreign country. Two of the states are also bordered by the Gulf of Mexico. This activity will guide students in using an atlas or other reference books to find absolute and relative locations of sites within this region.

Objectives

Students will
1. label a map of the South Central States with major cities and physical features.
2. use relative location clues to identify cities, rivers, and bodies of water.
3. use absolute location clues to identify the states.

Materials: "Location in the South Central States" student activity sheets, colored pencils, atlas, reference books, textbooks, pencils

Procedure
1. Review the concepts of absolute and relative location. Locate the South Central States on the wall map.
2. Assign "Location in the South Central States" student activity sheet to be completed individually or with a partner. Remind students that all labeling of maps should be done in manuscript.
3. Students should write the names of the six bordering states on the lines provided and on the map in the correct locations.
4. Write the name of the foreign country on the blank and then on the map.
5. After students have identified the bodies of water and written them on the lines provided, they should label them on the map. Remind students to outline the rivers with a blue colored pencil.
6. In question 4, the answers should be written on the lines provided and then labeled on the map.
7. In number five, students are to identify the cities on the lines provided and label them on the map.

Physical Features of the South Central States

The South Central States have physical characteristics that help to divide them into physical regions. This activity will discuss some of the major characteristics. The states are very diverse in landforms, ranging from low marshlands to scattered mountain ranges. This variety of landforms has a dramatic impact on the type of agriculture that is found throughout the region. Water also plays an important part in the physical makeup of this region. Both the Gulf of Mexico and major river systems help to make certain areas distinctly different from the dry rolling plains of the west. Students will look at these physical features and how they help to shape the lives of the people living there.

Objectives
Students will
1. read a description of major physical features of the South Central States.
2. label a map showing the location of major physical features.
3. read a book that illustrates some of these features.
4. role-play taking a trip through some of the regions and describe what they would expect to see.

Materials: "Physical Features of the South Central States" student activity sheets, reference books, paper, colored pencils, pencils, copy of *The Armadillo from Amarillo* by Lynn Cherry

Procedure
1. Discuss what physical features are and how they affect the lives of the people living near them.
2. Read "Physical Features of the South Central States" student activity sheets. Discuss each physical feature (region) that is mentioned.
3. Students should answer the questions in Part I as a review of the printed material. Go over the answers in class.
4. Students should label all of the physical features mentioned in question 1 under Part II on the map. Remind students that all labeling should be printed, and colored pencils should be used to do any necessary shading.
5. The book *The Armadillo from Amarillo* may be read aloud in class or, if sufficient copies are available, allow students to read it silently. After the reading, discuss the physical regions the armadillo crosses in his journey. Make reference to the map on the inside covers for assistance. Students should then role-play making a similar journey through some of the regions of the South Central States. As they write about their trip, they should record the types of scenery they would expect to see. Have reference books available that will allow students to see pictures of various landforms and regions within the South Central States.

Agriculture in the South Central States

The South Central States are important because of their agricultural production. Since the soil and climate vary in this region, the types of crops raised also vary. Traditionally, cotton was a major product and still remains one of the important crops, but the production has decreased in the past years. Sugar cane, rice, winter wheat, and sorghum grain are among the important agricultural products. The crops grown demonstrate how people have adapted to their environment with the farming methods used. Closely related to these crops is the beef cattle industry. Grazing land allows large numbers of cattle to be raised throughout the area. This industry is very important, especially in Texas and Oklahoma. This activity will allow students to gain an insight into the variety of agricultural products that come from the South Central States.

Objectives
Students will
1. read about major agricultural products being produced in the South Central States.
2. discuss methods of preventing soil erosion.
3. create an agricultural products map.
4. research the tradition of rodeos and their close relationship to the beef cattle industry.

Materials: "Agriculture in the South Central States" student activity sheets, poster board, chart paper, color markers, pencils, paper, drawing paper, crayons

Procedure
1. Ask the class to brainstorm a list of agricultural products that might be associated with the South Central States. Compile the list on chart paper. After compiling the list, read "Agriculture in the South Central States" student activity sheets to verify the list. If a crop is not mentioned in the selection, check reference books to see if it is grown in the area.
2. Students should answer the questions listed in Part I as a review of the reading. Discuss the questions in class. Discuss the importance of preventing soil erosion, especially in dry areas. Ask students to make suggestions of methods other than the one listed in the selection that might work in the region.
3. Divide the class into small groups. Each group should create an agricultural products map for one of the South Central States. The map should be cut out of a piece of poster board. The symbols may be drawn on drawing paper, colored, and then pasted on the map. Make certain that each group creates a legend or key for its map. The groups should be given time to share their creations with the class.
4. The final activity of researching the rodeo may be done individually or in small groups. Reports should be shared with the class. A compiled list of events may be posted in the class on chart paper. Lead the class into understanding that many of the events are based on actual jobs that are done as part of cattle ranching.

Urban Areas of the South Central States

Themes of Geography: Human-Environment Interaction, Movement

The South Central States region, like all regions of the United States, has seen the growth of major cities. The growth of cities is a prime example of human-environment interaction. Land is cleared for construction, roads are built, and parking lots are paved. Several major cities with interesting histories are located in the South Central States. Many of these cities contain aspects of cultures from other countries, such as France or Spain. While the growth of cities may offer many positive advantages, it also may cause serious problems that must be resolved. Finding solutions to all these problems will be one of the major tasks facing the people of these states in the future.

Objectives

Students will
1. read short selections about five major cities of the South Central States.
2. identify the cities using clues about their histories.
3. organize material into a chart.
4. research additional cities and chart basic information.

Materials: "Urban Areas of the South Central States" student activity sheets, reference books, paper, pencils

Procedure
1. Discuss how the growth of cities is a good example of human-environment interaction. Ask students to list examples of this theme found in a city.
2. Read "Urban Areas of the South Central States" student activity sheets. Discuss the background material given on each city. Note the strong French and Spanish influence in this region.
3. Students should complete the activity in Part I by writing the name of the city next to the clue that is given.
4. Students are to organize the information given in the selection by completing the chart in Part II. Stress to students that organizing information in such a manner is a good study skill.
5. Students may work with a partner or in small groups to find information about other cities in this region. They should decide ahead of time what information they want to include on their chart. The completed charts should be shared with the class.

The Oklahoma Land Run

Themes of Geography: Human-Environment Interaction, Movement

It began with a bugle call and a pistol shot. It was the largest migration in the history of the United States. In one day, nearly 60,000 people moved into what is now Oklahoma. This massive movement was destined to cause trouble as the people began to settle into their new homes. This activity will encourage students to consider some of the consequences that would have arisen due to this large-scale movement of people. As students consider problems that must have been created, they will also try to find some possible solutions. This event in American history shows the effect of movement on those who moved and those who were already in the territory.

Objectives
Students will
1. read the story of the Oklahoma Land Run.
2. brainstorm to consider both positive and negative consequences of such an event.
3. suggest possible solutions to the problems caused by such an event.

Materials: "The Oklahoma Land Run" student activity sheets, chart paper, pencils, colored markers

Procedure
1. Discuss the geographic theme of movement in class. Stress that when movement takes place, people carry cultural baggage with them. Ask students to identify some examples of cultural baggage and how this baggage affects both the people moving and those already living there.
2. Read "The Oklahoma Land Run" student activity sheets. Help the class realize the size of this massive movement of people in a short period. Ask students to be thinking of possible problems as the selection is read.
3. After the selection is read, discuss the role of the Native Americans in this event. In what ways were their lives probably changed forever?
4. Students should answer the questions in Part I as a review of the printed materials. Go over the answers in class.
5. Students should work in small groups to complete the activity in Part II. Each group should list as many consequences as possible, classifying them as either positive or negative. Then, the groups should list specific problems that they feel must have occurred because of the movement. Finally, they should list possible solutions for one or more of the problems. The lists should be written on chart paper and placed on the wall as each group reports to the large group.
6. Ask the class to think about migrations occurring today. Would the same problems be present, or would there be a different set? What solutions might be used to solve the problems today?

Conclusion

The South Central States have a rich history. They have been influenced by many cultures, each of which has left its mark on the multicultural society that now exists. Great challenges lie ahead of the states as they continue to see urban growth taking place. New jobs and housing must be found to make room for the new people coming to the area. The governments must begin to take action now to provide the needed solutions. The South Central States face many challenges in the future, but they have been able to overcome many in the past. This study will provide a good glimpse of a region of comparisons and contrasts.

Location in the South Central States

The South Central States region includes the four states of Texas, Oklahoma, Louisiana, and Arkansas. The activities below will help to locate this region using both relative and absolute location. Answer each of the following questions using an atlas, textbook, or other reference materials.

1. Write the names of the six states that border the South Central States on the blanks below. Then label each of them on the map above.

    a. _____   b. _____

    c. _____   d. _____

    e. _____   f. _____

2. _____is the foreign country that borders this region to the southwest. Write the name of this country on the map above.

3. Several bodies of water help to mark the borders in this region. Identify each of the following rivers or gulfs by using the relative location clues. Locate each of these bodies of water on the map. Outline them with a blue colored pencil and write their names in the appropriate places.

    a. This large body of water marks the southern border of Louisiana and the southeast border of Texas. _____

    b. This river, which begins in Colorado, helps to form the border between the United States and Mexico. _____

c. This river, which is surrounded by rich farm land, forms the border between Texas and Oklahoma. _____

d. This river forms the eastern border of Arkansas and Louisiana and the western border of Tennessee and Mississippi. _____

4. Using an atlas, identify the states in which the following coordinates would be found:
   a. 35° N and 93° W   _____
   b. 36° N and 98° W   _____
   c. 30° N and 91° W   _____
   d. 28° N and 98° W   _____

5. Identify the following cities based on the clues given below. Then use the clues to help label the cities on the map.

   a. west Texas city near border of Mexico located at 31° 47' N and 106° 27' W

   _____

   b. city in southeast Texas near Galveston Bay located at 29° 46' N and 95° 21' W

   _____

   c. city in Louisiana located south of Lake Pontchartrain and about 100 miles (160 kilometers) from the Gulf of Mexico _____

   d. city in northeastern Oklahoma located along the Arkansas River about 100 miles (160 kilometers) from the Mississippi River

   _____

   e. cities located about 30 miles from each other in the northeastern region of Texas

   _____ and _____

   f. capital city of Arkansas located in the south central region of the state

   _____

   g. Texas city located in the panhandle between New Mexico and Oklahoma

   _____

   h. capital city of Oklahoma located in the central region of the state

   _____

   i. Texas capital city located in the south central region of the state

   _____

   j. Texas city located southwest of Austin

   _____

   k. capital city of Louisiana located northwest of Lake Pontchartrain

   _____

Physical Features of the South Central States

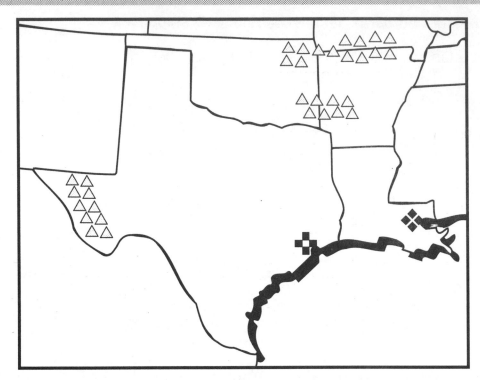

The South Central States are characterized by landforms that range from low marshlands along the Gulf Coast to high plains and finally scattered mountain ranges. Rolling grasslands and valleys make up a large part of the region.

The Gulf Coastal Plain extends all along the Gulf of Mexico across Louisiana and down the east shore of Texas. In south Texas, the plains extend over to the Rio Grande River. Low marshland regions are found along the coast. The Mississippi River Delta is included in the marshlands of southeastern Louisiana.

A *delta* is formed from the flow of a river. Rivers usually empty into a larger body of water such as an ocean or gulf. A *gulf* is a part of the ocean that pushes into the land. As a river flows, it carries fine soil called *silt*. As the river reaches its mouth at the larger body of water, the flow of the water slows down. The soil carried by the water falls to the bottom of the river. Eventually, this soil will build up at the mouth to form a delta.

The Mississippi Delta covers an area of 13,000 square miles (33,700 square kilometers). This is one fourth of the total land area of Louisiana. It is the most fertile soil found in the state. The silt carried by the river has raised the riverbeds. This means that the Mississippi River is actually higher than surrounding backlands. This makes the threat of floods a very real problem. *Bayous*, slow-moving inlets or outlets of rivers and lakes, are the chief natural drains of overflow water. In addition, people have built *levees* along the river to help provide flood control.

The land of the South Central States rises to mountains in three major areas. The Guadalupe Mountains rise in the western region of Texas between the Rio Grande River and New Mexico. Guadalupe Peak, 8,751 feet (2,667 meters) is the highest point in Texas. The Ouachita Mountains stretch from eastern Oklahoma to central Arkansas. These mountains run generally east and west. Blue Mountain, 2,623 feet (799 meters) is the highest peak. The Ozark Plateau (mountains) also extends into the northwestern part of Arkansas and the northeastern region of Oklahoma. Rugged hills, deep valleys, and swift rivers are features of this region. Forests cover much of the Ozarks.

The Great Plains region stretches from southwest Texas across Oklahoma. These plains actually include a series of dry, treeless plains in the central part of the United States and Canada. The plains extend 2,500 miles (4,020 kilometers) from Texas to Alberta, Canada. They extend from the Rocky Mountains to the eastern regions of Nebraska and Oklahoma for approximately 400 miles (640 kilometers). One part of the Great Plains in Texas is called *Leano Estacado*. *Leano Estacado* is Spanish for "staked plain." The name was given because early Spanish explorers found the land so flat that the only way they could find their way was to put stakes in the ground to show where they had been.

Several major rivers are found in the South Central States. Many of these rivers help to form the borders between states. The Mississippi River stretches for 2,348 miles (3,778 kilometers) across the central part of the United States. It forms the eastern border of Arkansas and most of Louisiana. It is a major transportation route and is the busiest inland waterway. Barges can travel from the Gulf of Mexico to as far north as Minneapolis, Minnesota.

The Rio Grande River forms the international border between the United States and Mexico for a distance of 1,240 miles (1,996 kilometers). From its source high in the Rocky Mountains of Colorado, the river flows 1,885 miles (3,033 kilometers) to the Gulf of Mexico. The river bears a Spanish name which means "Great River."

The Arkansas River is a tributary of the Mississippi River. The river runs through Oklahoma and Arkansas on its way to the Mississippi. Barges can travel up the river as far as Tulsa, Oklahoma. Thus, the inland city of Tulsa is a major port city.

The Red River travels through all of the South Central States. The river rises in north Texas near the city of Amarillo and helps to form the border between Texas and Oklahoma. It flows for 1,300 miles (2,090 kilometers) before emptying into the Mississippi. The name of the river comes from the red silt that it carries. Rich farm land may be found on both sides of the river.

Lake Pontchartrain is part of the 3,400 square miles (8,810 square kilometers) of inland water in Louisiana. The 626-square-mile (1,619 square kilometers) lake of brackish water is the largest in the state. *Brackish* water means that it is part saltwater. Many of the saltwater lakes in the state were once extensions of the sea that were eventually cut off by ridges of sand or deposits of silt.

Student Activities

Part I. Answer each of the following questions
1. The _____ extends all along the Gulf of Mexico across Louisiana and down the east shore of Texas.
2. Explain how a delta is formed. _____
   _____
   _____
3. What percent of the total area of Louisiana is covered with the Mississippi Delta?
   _____
4. What are bayous, and how do they help control flooding?
   _____
   _____
5. How have people tried to control the flooding of the Mississippi? _____
   _____
6. What three areas of highlands (mountains) are found in the South Central States?
   _____, _____, _____
7. The _____ is a dry, treeless plain in the central part of the United States and Canada.
8. Four major rivers found in the South Central States include _____,
   _____, _____, and _____.
9. Lake _____is a large brackish lake in Louisiana.

Part II. Complete the following activities.
1. Use the map of the South Central States to label the following physical features: Gulf Coastal Plain, Red River, Arkansas River, Rio Grande, Mississippi River, Lake Pontchartrain, Great Plains, Guadalupe Mountains, Ouachita Mountains, Ozark Plateau, Galveston Bay, Gulf of Mexico, and the Mississippi Delta.

2. Read the book *The Armadillo from Amarillo* by Lynn Cherry. This book gives a beautiful illustration of the physical regions that are traveled through. Choose one of the physical regions of this area and role-play that you are traveling there. Write a description of what you would expect to see.

Agriculture in the South Central States

The types of crops grown in the South Central States are directly related to the climate and soil types found in the region. Because of the varied climate and soil conditions, a large variety of crops are found in these states. These crops include soybeans, rice, sugar cane, cotton, sweet potatoes, citrus fruits, vegetables, winter wheat, and sorghum grain.

Sorghum grain comes from any of a group of tall grassy plants that look similar to the corn plant. Sorghum grain is an important crop worldwide and is used in the making of syrup, as feed for livestock, and in the manufacturing of brooms and brushes. Sorghum grain is raised in Texas, Oklahoma, and Arkansas. Texas is the leading production state.

The amount of cotton produced has been decreasing over the past 50 years in the United States. This decrease was caused by pests, such as the boll weevil; foreign competition; expensive mechanization; and synthetic fibers. Most of the cotton today is grown on large irrigated and mechanized farms. Texas is the leading cotton-producing state.

The subtropical climate of the lower delta area of Louisiana is very important to the raising of sugar cane. When sugar cane is harvested, the roots remain in the ground. As long as it does not frost, the roots will continue to grow plants each year without replanting. The Louisiana Delta area often goes several years in a row without a frost. When the sugar cane is harvested, it is cut, washed, and crushed. Cane syrup and sugar are made from the sugar cane.

Rice is an important crop, especially in the states of Arkansas, Louisiana, and Texas. Arkansas is the leading rice-producing state. To grow well, rice must have warm temperatures and plenty of moisture. Even though most of the rice-growing areas get 40 inches or more of rain, more water is needed. Rice fields are usually irrigated so that sufficient water is available. Most of the rice grown in Arkansas is in the Mississippi Alluvial Plain, which uses the Mississippi River as a source of water. Some farmers even flood their rice fields and raise fish in them.

Winter wheat is an important crop in Oklahoma and Texas. Winter wheat is planted in the fall. The roots grow strong before the cold winter weather begins. The warm temperatures of the spring cause the wheat to grow rapidly. It is harvested in the early summer. The roots of the wheat are an important weapon against soil erosion. In areas of little rain, roots help to keep the soil from blowing away. Oklahoma is one of the major wheat-producing states.

The raising of beef cattle is important in all four of the South Central States. In Texas, the production of beef cattle is the largest source of farm income, providing about 60 percent of the annual total. Texas is the leading beef cattle-producing state. The climate is so mild in much of Texas that the cattle can graze outdoors all year long, making the raising of cattle cheaper. Before sending the cattle to markets, they are often sent to *feedlots*. Here they are fed special diets that add pounds. When the cattle have gained enough weight, they are sold for meat.

Student Activities

Part I. Answer the following questions about agriculture in the South Central States.

1. What physical geographic factors directly affect the types and amounts of crops grown in the South Central States? _____

2. What is sorghum grain, and how is it used? _____

_____

3. Why would this sorghum grain be important in the South Central States? _____

_____

4. What role do feedlots play in the production of beef cattle? _____

_____

5. How is winter wheat a weapon against soil erosion? _____

_____

6. What factors have caused a reduction in the production of cotton over the past years?

_____

7. Which crop that is raised in the South Central States needs a frost-free climate for best results? _____

Part II. Complete the following activities.

1. Create an agricultural products map. Draw or trace the outline of one of the South Central States onto a piece of poster board. Cut out the state. Research to find the major agricultural products of the state and where they are produced. Draw a symbol for each product and place the symbol on the map in the region where the crop is grown. Remember that you may need several symbols, because the product may be raised in several regions. Finally, make a map key by listing the products on a sheet of drawing paper and drawing the representative symbol next to each product. Make a presentation of your map to the class.

2. Rodeos are a colorful part of U.S. heritage. Research rodeos to find out how they were started. Include in your report the various events that are staged at a rodeo. How are these events related to the beef cattle industry?

Urban Areas of the South Central States

Several major cities have emerged in the South Central States. Five of the largest are Houston, Dallas, San Antonio, New Orleans, and Fort Worth. Each city has a unique history and is making a special contribution to the region.

Houston is the largest city in Texas. It has a population of nearly 1.7 million people and covers an area of 556 square miles. It is generally known as the oil capital of the United States and the home of Johnson Space Center. Founded in 1836 and incorporated in 1837, the city is named in honor of Sam Houston, the hero of the Texan War of Independence against Mexico. Much of the economy still reflects San Antonio's status as an oil city. Major industries include oil refineries, chemical plants, and oil equipment manufacturing facilities.

Dallas and Fort Worth are cities 30 miles apart and are often grouped together as one metropolitan area. Dallas has a population of just over one million people and covers an area of 378 square miles (979 square kilometers). The city was founded in 1841 and incorporated in 1871. Dallas is nicknamed the "Big D." It began as a railroad shipping center for cattle and cotton. Major industries in Dallas include electronics, banking, insurance, and fashion. Dallas remains one of the major transportation hubs of the United States.

Fort Worth began as a military post in 1849 and was incorporated as a city in 1873. Fort Worth has a population of 447,619 and covers 251 square miles (650 square kilometers). From the beginning, the city was a center for cattle marketing and was often referred to as "Cowtown." In 1917 oil was discovered in the area. Today Fort Worth is noted for industries including petroleum, grain, and aerospace. It also has maintained its animal stockyards. Located between the cities of Dallas and Fort Worth is one of the busiest airports in the United States.

San Antonio was the site of a Spanish garrison in 1718. It gained fame as the site of the Battle of the Alamo during the Texas War for Independence in 1836. In 1837 Texas became an independent nation and San Antonio was incorporated as a city. The city has a population of 935,393 and covers an area of 328 square miles (850 square kilometers). Today, the military, health care, and tourism contribute heavily to San Antonio's economy. San Antonio ranks as one of the leading convention cities in the southwestern part of the United States. Major industries include aircraft parts, clothing, electronic products, food products, fertilizer, medical supplies, oil field equipment, and petroleum products.

New Orleans was founded by the French in 1718. The United States purchased the city with the Louisiana Purchase in 1803. It was incorporated as a city in 1805. New Orleans is the oldest city in the South Central States. The city has a population of 496,938 and covers an area of 364 square miles (943 square kilometers). Located on the Mississippi River about 100 miles (160 kilometers) from the Gulf of Mexico, the city is a leading port of the United States. It has become a major oil tanker port. Major industries include petroleum, chemicals, metal products, and tourism.

The growth of urban centers in the South Central States has not been without the creation of problems that must be addressed in the future. Some of these include traffic congestion, air pollution, ghetto growth, and housing shortages. The influx of people has also put a strain on public facilities such as schools, water supplies, and public transportation. The solutions to these problems remain a challenge for the future.

Student Activities

Part I. Identify each of the following cities located in the South Central States by using the clues given from the selection above.

_____ 1. The largest city in the state of Texas.

_____ 2. The oldest city in the South Central States.

_____ 3. The city known as "Cowtown."

_____ 4. The home of the Alamo.

_____ 5. Nicknamed the "Big D."

_____ 6. Founded by the French in 1718, it is now one of the major port cities in the United States.

_____ 7. Named after a Texas hero, the city is known as the oil capital of the United States.

_____ 8. Begun as a military post in 1849, this city remains a center for cattle marketing.

_____ 9. This city began as the site of a Spanish garrison and has become one of the leading convention cities in the United States.

_____ 10. Begun in 1841 as a railroad shipping center, this city continues to be a major transportation hub.

Part II. Complete the following activities.

1. The growth of urban areas in a region is an example of the geographic themes of human-environment interaction and movement. However, in both themes, when change occurs, there is a price to be paid. Work in small groups to discuss the problems being raised by the growth of cities in the South Central States as given in the selection just read. Role-play a committee that has been appointed to solve these problems within the next ten years. List each problem on a piece of chart paper and then brainstorm for possible solutions. After the brainstorming session, discuss the solutions and rank them in the order of probable success. Present your findings to the class. The entire class should come to a consensus on the best plan to combat each problem.

2. Organizing information is an important skill to develop. Use the information given in the selection to complete this chart.

City	Date Founded	Date Incorporated	Area	Major Industries

3. There are other important cities in the South Central States, including El Paso, Austin, Oklahoma City, Tulsa, and Little Rock. Work in small groups to research each of these cities. Combine the information you find and present it on a chart to share with the class. The headings may be the same of those on the chart above, or you may decide on other topics.

The Oklahoma Land Run

It began with a bugle call at noon on April 22, 1889, and the firing of a pistol. That call sent thousands of settlers racing across the plains of the "Indian Territory," which is now called Oklahoma. Never before in American history had there been such a migration of people at one time. In a single day, more than 60,000 settlers moved into the Indian Territory.

After 1819, the federal government began trying to get the Indian tribes of the southeastern United States to move into the Oklahoma area. After struggles and hardships, the "Five Civilized Tribes"—the Cherokee, Chickasaw, Choctaw, Creek, and Seminole—moved to Oklahoma. They were promised all the land of present-day Oklahoma except the panhandle.

At the close of the Civil War, Congress forced the tribes to give up the western part of their land because they had supported the South. The land that bordered the Indian Territory filled up rapidly. Soon there was no more free or cheap land available. Many cattlemen crossed through the Indian Territory on their way to cattle markets in Kansas. They saw the fertile grazing land and wanted to have access to it. One group of cattlemen leased more than six million acres (2.4 million hectares) from the Indians for a period of five years. However, the United States Government declared the lease void and ordered the cattle removed.

Cattlemen in the area began to urge the United States Government to open part of the land for settlement. The government finally agreed to take action. It bought over three million acres (1.2 million hectares) from the Creek and Seminole tribes. Authorities declared almost 1,900,000 acres (769,000 hectares) open for settlement, beginning at noon on April 22, 1889.

On the morning of the great run, the settlers came on horses, in wagons, on bicycles, on foot, and by train to stake their claims to the farmlands and town lots that were available. The army kept them back behind a line until noon. At noon a bugle blew and a pistol was fired to begin the rush. The settlers began a race to claim the best sites. In all, about 50,000 people moved into Oklahoma in that one day. Gutherie and Oklahoma City became cities of more than 10,000 people each on that day.

The settlers were referred to as "Sooners," because some of them were on the land sooner than it was actually open. Because of the limited amount of land, settlers usually carried weapons to defend their claims. Some of the settlers who went into the territory before the legal time ran their horses hard just before noon so they could prove that they had indeed just arrived at their site.

The Territory of Oklahoma was created by Congress in May 1890 with Gutherie as the capital. At the same time, the panhandle was added to the territory. George W. Steele was appointed as the first territorial governor.

During the 1890s, more and more Indians began to accept individual ownership of land rather than land being owned by the tribe. Eventually, land not owned by tribal members began to be opened for settlement. Some of this land was distributed by a rush and other land was distributed by a lottery. The greatest opening occurred on September 16, 1893. The Cherokee Outlet in north central Oklahoma and the Tonkawa and Pawnee reservations were opened. Over 50,000 people claimed land in the 6.5 million-acre (2.6 million hectares) area on the first day.

In 1907, the Oklahoma Territory and the Indian Territories, with a combined population of about 1.5 million people, joined to become Oklahoma, the forty-sixth state admitted to the United States.

Student Activities

Part I. Answer the following questions about the Oklahoma Land Run.

1. Name the "Five Civilized Tribes" moved to Oklahoma by the United States Government. _____, _____,
_____,_____, and _____

2. Why were the tribes forced to give up some of their land after the Civil War?

   _____

3. What caused the settlers to begin urging the government to open the Indian land for settlement? _____

4. When was the Oklahoma Territory established, and who was its first governor?

   _____   _____

5. What two territories joined in 1907 to become the forty-sixth state?

   _____ and _____

Part II. Complete the following activity.

The Oklahoma Land Run was one of the largest single-day migrations in history. Work in small groups to discuss the positive and negative consequences of such a massive movement of people. Consider such factors as these: problems that would face the settlers, the effect on the Indian tribes, and the problems of governing the new territories. Write your findings on chart paper to present to the class. Choose one of the problems that your group listed and think of possible solutions.

The Rocky Mountain States

Goals for This Unit

Students will
1. use absolute and relative location clues to identify sites and label maps.
2. label on a map the major physical regions included in the Rocky Mountain States.
3. research and map the major national parks located in the Rocky Mountain States.
4. create a journal about the workers constructing the transcontinental railroad.
5. research and illustrate various methods of irrigation.
6. compare three major cities of the Rocky Mountain States and discuss problems caused by urbanization in the region.
7. write dramatic monologues about the lives of Native-American leaders.
8. create collages to depict Native-American life before and after the settlement of the West.

Rationale

The area known as the Rocky Mountain States is really three separate physical regions in one. This unit will look at all three regions. This section of the United States has the heritage of being the Old West. Many Native-American reservations are found in the area, along with a strong Spanish influence in the southern areas. The region provides an interesting study of a region that is having to grow with a limited supply of water. Much of the agriculture that occurs in this area is there because of irrigation. Combine this water shortage with the growth of urbanization in selected areas, and the problems begin to be of major concern. This study will look at these problems and challenge students to search for possible solutions for the future.

Skills Taught in This Unit

labeling maps
using absolute and relative location
brainstorming
organizing information into charts
writing dramatic monologues

using atlases
writing journals
designing posters
making a collage

Vocabulary

continental steppe climate	Chinook	Continental Divide
tree line	basin	plateau
Four Corners	rain shadow	geysers
parks	mesas	hogans
aquifer	irrigation	tepees

Background Material

The study of the Rocky Mountain States is actually a study of three physical regions—the Great Plains, the Rocky Mountains, and the Intermountain Region. All three regions are different, yet they have a great deal in common. This study will look at some of the problems being faced by this region and encourage students to think about possible solutions. The major problems facing the region include a shortage of water and growing urban areas. These are problems that are not strangers to other parts of the world. A study of these states will provide an opportunity to look to preparing for the future.

Location in the Rocky Mountain States

Themes of Geography: Location

The Rocky Mountain States region is composed of eight states. Within these states are several major cities and towns. Absolute and relative location allow students to pinpoint where sites are located. This activity will give students practice in using both absolute and relative location clues to correctly identify and label a map of the region. An atlas, reference books, or textbooks will be needed to help students correctly identify each site.

Objectives

Students will
1. locate major cities and towns using absolute and relative location clues.
2. locate and identify the states in the Rocky Mountain region by absolute and relative location clues.
3. label a map showing the location of states, cities, and towns in the Rocky Mountain States region.

Materials: "Location in the Rocky Mountain States" student activity sheets, pencils, atlases, reference books, colored pencils

Procedure

1. Introduce the Rocky Mountain States region by identifying the states and locating them on a wall map of the United States.
2. Conduct a brief review of absolute and relative location and how they help to pinpoint the location of a site.
3. Read the introductory paragraph of "Location in the Rocky Mountain States" student activity sheets. Remind students that labeling on a map should be done in manuscript. Colored pencils should be used to shade in or trace areas on a map.
4. Students may work individually or with a partner as they go through the activity sheets. Atlases and other reference books should be available in the class or in an area nearby.
5. Remind students that answers should be written in appropriate blanks on the activity pages and then labeled on the map.

Physical Features of the Rocky Mountain States

The Rocky Mountain States are actually made up of several different physical regions, ranging from plains to plateaus to high mountains. The three major regions are the Great Plains, the Rocky Mountains, and the Intermountain Region. The Great Plains are located between the Central Plains and the Rocky Mountains. They cover the eastern part of Montana, Wyoming, Colorado, and New Mexico and the western part of Texas, Oklahoma, Kansas, Nebraska, South Dakota, and North Dakota. These plains gradually rise to meet the mountains. The Rocky Mountains are the next major region. There are actually several smaller ranges that make up the Rockies. There are many peaks above 12,000 feet (3,659 meters) in this region. The Intermountain Region lies between the Rocky Mountains and the Sierra Nevada and Cascade Mountains. This region stretches from the Colorado Plateau to the Great Basin to the Columbia Plateau. The physical features of this region are varied. This activity will introduce students to these major physical regions of the Rocky Mountain States.

Objectives

Students will

1. discuss the physical features of the various regions making up the Rocky Mountain States.
2. define key geographic terms.
3. label the major physical regions of the Rocky Mountain States.
4. identify major national parks found in this region.

Materials: "Physical Features of the Rocky Mountain States" student activity sheets, reference books, atlases, pencils, colored pencils, chart paper, color markers

Procedure

1. Locate the Rocky Mountain States on a wall map. Explain that there are several large physical regions included within this area. Explain that a physical region is a region that is different because of the land or other physical characteristics.
2. Look at a physical map of this area. By looking at the colors used on the key, ask students to identify some of the physical features found in these states. (Example: plains, plateaus, etc.)
3. Read "Physical Features of the Rocky Mountain States" student activity sheets. Discuss the three major physical regions mentioned in the selection. Brainstorm terms used to describe each region. List these terms on the board or on chart paper.
4. Students should answer the questions as a review of the material read. Go over the answers in class.
5. Remind students that all printing on maps should be done in manuscript. Also colored pencils should be used for shading or outlining. Assign students to complete the map activity in Part II. Atlases or other reference books will be needed to find the proper position for the terms on the map.
6. Completed maps should be displayed in the class.

Agriculture in the Rocky Mountain States

The study of agriculture in the Rocky Mountain States examines how man has found ways to provide water to dry land in sufficient quantities for crops to grow. For many years the Great Plains were used only for grazing, but today much of the beef-cattle ranching has been combined with wheat production. Water from the underground aquifers and rivers has provided the moisture needed to make this change. The story is much the same for the Intermountain Region. Cotton and vegetables are the two main irrigated crops in this region. Without water from the rivers, there would be little or no agriculture possible. Dams built on the rivers have allowed humans to control the flow of the water and harness it for both irrigation and hydroelectricity. The Central Arizona Project, for example, takes water from the Colorado River and sends it to Phoenix and Tucson. This activity will involve students in researching methods of irrigation that have helped the dry areas of the western United States become productive agricultural areas. It will also show that with this intervention on the part of humans comes the possibility of problems such as the falling water levels of the Ogallala aquifer. These problems must be addressed or the agriculture may cease.

Objectives
Students will
1. discuss the physical resources that have allowed agriculture to grow in areas of the Rocky Mountain States.
2. research methods of irrigation used today.
3. identify potential problems with the continued dependence on irrigation around the world and suggest possible solutions to these problems.

Materials: "Agriculture in the Rocky Mountain States" student activity sheets, chart paper, paper, color markers, poster board, crayons, tape, reference books

Procedure
1. Discuss ways people change their environment to improve their way of life. Include in the discussion ways people use water to allow for agriculture.
2. Read "Agriculture in the Rocky Mountain States" student activity sheets. Discuss the emphasis that is placed on water in this region. Students need to understand that, without irrigation, there would be little or no agriculture.
3. Assign the questions to be answered under Part I. Go over the questions as a review of the material just read.
4. In the first activity in Part II, students will need to conduct research to identify the various methods of irrigation that are used. A good supply of reference books and magazines, such as *National Geographic*, should be available for use. The posters may be created using drawings to illustrate the methods of irrigation, or pictures of various methods may be cut out and pasted on the poster board. Remind students to print neatly when labeling the illustrations on the poster.

5. Students will need to work in small groups to complete the second activity. Each group will brainstorm to find possible problems arising from the increase in dependency on irrigated land for farming around the world. Ask them to be specific when they list potential problems. After the problems are listed, each group should then seek to list possible solutions to the problems. Each group will need time to report its work to the rest of the class.

Urban Areas of the Rocky Mountain States

Themes of Geography: Human-Environment Interaction, Region

The area known as the Rocky Mountain States is often referred to as the empty region of the United States. However, there are many areas of urban growth that are located in this section. This activity will look at three such cities—Denver from the Great Plains, Phoenix from the Intermountain Region, and Salt Lake City from the Rocky Mountains. Each of these cities has many common characteristics, but they are also very different. Students will read about the history and economy of each city. In addition, emphasis is placed on the potential problems that could arise with future urban growth in a region that has limited water supplies.

Objectives
Students will
1. read about three representative cities from the physical regions of the Rocky Mountain States.
2. create a model city that would take into consideration problems that might arise because of further urbanization in an area with limited water.
3. organize information into a chart comparing the three cities being studied.

Materials: "Urban Areas of the Rocky Mountain States" student activity sheets, drawing paper, poster board, color markers, pencils, paper, chart paper

Procedure
1. Discuss urbanization and what is needed to make a city grow and prosper. Make a list of these needs on the board or on chart paper to display in the class.
2. Read "Urban Areas of the Rocky Mountain States" student activity sheets. Talk about the three cities mentioned and reasons for their growth.
3. Ask students to work individually on finding the correct answers to the clues under Part I. These may be discussed in class as a review of the material just read.
4. In preparing to do the first activity in Part II, students should refer to the list of things needed to make a city grow. This will be helpful as they discuss their own city. In each small group, students should make a list of potential problems for urban growth in the Rocky Mountain States.
5. The group should then plan a city of the future that will take these problems into consideration and try to plan for them. Each group should draw its city on a sheet of poster board. Explanations of how the plan will help to avoid potential problems should be written out for each part of the city.

6. Each group should share its plan with the rest of the class.
7. In the second activity, students may work individually or with a partner. Remind students that organizing material into charts is a technique that will help them in studying large amounts of material. Each student or group should decide on topics to be compared and then make a chart showing the comparison. The charts should be done on chart paper and displayed in the classroom.

Native Americans in the Rocky Mountain States

Themes of Geography: Human-Environment Interaction, Region

The Native Americans have made many contributions to the culture of the United States. These contributions are clearly seen in the Rocky Mountain States, where large numbers of Native Americans still live. The early tribes were essentially either farmers or nomadic hunters and gatherers. Each group made its own distinct contributions to our society. This activity will look at four of the tribes currently located in the Rocky Mountain States. It will show how they have changed since the settlement of the West. Many of the tribes are still living on reservations set aside for them by the U.S. Government. Some of the tribes now own their own industries that are operated on the reservation. Life has changed but there are still many problems to be faced in the future.

Objectives

Students will
1. identify and discuss the history of four tribes living in the Rocky Mountain States.
2. research the life of one great Native-American leader and role-play a first-person monologue describing his or her life.
3. create two collages showing the life of a selected Native-American tribe as it was before and after the settlement of the West by whites.

Materials: "Native Americans in the Rocky Mountain States" student activity sheets, paper, pencils, chart paper, color markers, poster board, reference books, textbook

Procedure

1. Introduce the lesson by asking the class to brainstorm contributions made by Native Americans to our society. List these contributions on a sheet of chart paper and display it on the wall.
2. Read "Native Americans in the Rocky Mountain States" student activity sheets. As the sheets are read, students should begin to draw comparisons between life of the Native Americans now and the way it was before the white settlers came.
3. Hold a discussion of the material, especially the way the settlement of the area has affected the lives of Native Americans.

4. As a review of the material, students should complete the activity under Part I. Go over this in class when all are finished.
5. Introduce students to the two Native-American leaders mentioned in the selection. Then point out the list of other leaders in activity 1 under Part II. Each student should choose a leader to research. Each student should then write a first-person monologue about his or her life to share with the class. Making costumes for the event would make it even more interesting.
6. Students should work in small groups to complete the second activity. Each group will need two sheets of poster board, colored markers, and reference books. One collage should be titled "Traditional Life" and the other "Modern Life." Each collage may be made by pasting pictures on the poster board and labeling it or by making drawings to go on the board. Each group should make a presentation of its tribe to the class.

Conclusion

The Rocky Mountain States region is composed of three main physical sections. The states are united in a common heritage of the Old West. They also have—to some extent—a common problem, a shortage of water. Cooperation among the states will be needed in solving this problem. The people must begin to work together to plan for the future in ways that will maximize the wise use of available water sources. How well the states are able to do this will help determine how much progress and growth will be seen in this region.

Location in the Rocky Mountain States

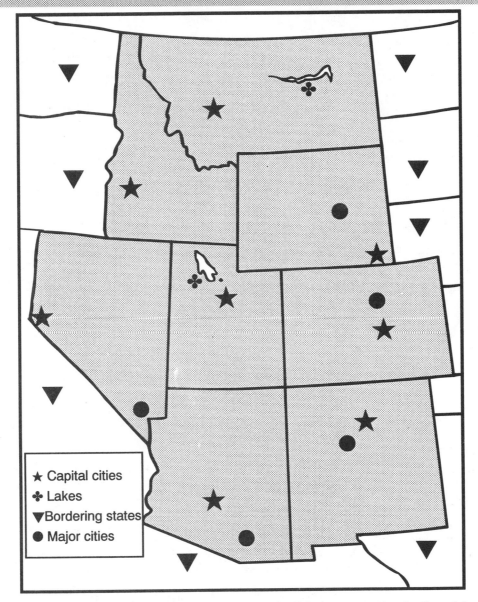

★ Capital cities
✿ Lakes
▼ Bordering states
● Major cities

The Rocky Mountain States region is made up of eight states, including Montana, Idaho, Wyoming, Nevada, Utah, Colorado, Arizona, and New Mexico. The area is sometimes referred to as the "Old West." The Rocky Mountain States actually contain three distinct regions. The Great Plains Region is made up of flatlands. It is a section noted for dust storms, blizzards, and droughts. The Rocky Mountain region is the watershed for the western United States. Its rivers supply water for surrounding states and it is rich in natural resources. The Intermountain Region is made up of deserts, mountains, and canyons. This region is rich in minerals. There is a long history of Indian and Spanish settlements in this region. Water is a vital resource for this area.

Student Activities

Using atlases or other resource books, use the absolute and relative location clues given below to answer each question. After the questions are answered, label the map on the previous page.

1. Using an atlas, find the names of the nine states that border the Rocky Mountain States. Write their names below and label these states on the map.

    a. _____   b. _____   c. _____
    d. _____   e. _____   f. _____
    g. _____   h. _____   i. _____

2. Name the country that borders this region on the south. _____

3. Name the three Canadian Provinces that border this region on the north.

    a. _____   b. _____   c. _____

4. Use the following absolute and relative locations clues to identify each of the states in the Rocky Mountain States region. Write the name of each state in the appropriate place on the map.

    a. _____ This state is located east of Washington and Oregon and south of British Columbia. It is located at 45° N and 115° W.

    b. _____ This state is located southwest of Nebraska, west of Kansas, and northwest of Oklahoma. It is located at 40° N and 105° W.

    c. _____ This state is southwest of Wyoming, south of Idaho, east of Nevada and north of Arizona. It is located at 40° N and 110° W.

    d. _____ This state is located north of Mexico, west of New Mexico, east of California, and south of Utah. It is located at 35° N and 110° W.

    e. _____ This state is located north of Wyoming, west of North Dakota and south of Saskatchewan and Alberta. It is located at 47° N and 110° W.

    f. _____ This state is located east of California, south of Oregon, northwest of Arizona, and west of Utah. It is located at 40° N and 117° W.

    g. _____ This state is located south of Montana, west of South Dakota, north of Colorado, and east of Idaho. It is located at 43° and 107° W.

    h. _____ This state is located east of Arizona, south of Colorado, north and west of Texas. It is located at 35° and 105° W.

5. Below are clues to help you identify the cities which appear on the map. Use atlases and reference books to help identify each city below and then label the city correctly on the map.

a._____ This capital city is located in north central New Mexico between the Pecos and Rio Grande Rivers.

b._____ This capital city sits on the western Continental Divide in west central Montana.

c._____ This capital city is located near the California border and Lake Tahoe. It is located south of Reno.

d._____ This capital city is located southeast of the Great Salt Lake and northeast of the city of Provo.

e._____ This city is located on the Rio Grande River southwest of Santa Fe.

f._____ This capital city is located near the Gila River in south central Arizona.

g._____ This capital city is located on the South Platte River about 10 miles (16 kilometers) east of the Rocky Mountains.

h._____ This capital city is located in the extreme southeast corner of Wyoming near the border of Colorado.

i._____ This city is located on the North Platte River northwest of the city of Cheyenne.

j._____ This city is located in the north central part of Colorado northwest of Denver and south of Fort Collins.

k._____ This city is located southeast of Phoenix near the Santa Cruz River in the southeastern part of Arizona.

l._____ This city is in the southeastern part of Nevada near Hoover Dam and Lake Mead.

m._____ This capital city of Idaho is located in the southwest section of the state near the border of Oregon.

6. Identify and label the following lakes on the map.

a._____ is formed behind the Fort Peck Dam on the Missouri River in Montana.

b._____ is a large saltwater lake in northwest Utah.

Physical Features of the Rocky Mountain States

The Rocky Mountain States are actually divided into three physical regions. Those regions are the Great Plains, the Rocky Mountains, and the Intermountain Region. Each region has distinct physical features.

The Great Plains are located in the middle of the United States between the Central Plains and the Rocky Mountains. They include the western parts of Texas, Oklahoma, Kansas, Nebraska, South Dakota, and North Dakota, and the eastern parts of New Mexico, Colorado, Wyoming, and Montana. These plains rise from east to west and reach as high as 4,000 feet (1,220 meters) above sea level.

This region has a *continental steppe climate* that features great extremes. A continental steppe climate goes from hot to cold with great changes in daily temperatures. There is generally little precipitation. The temperature range may be from -40° F (-40°C) in the winter to 100° F (38°C) in the summer. In the winter, blizzards with blowing snow may occur. In the summer, hot moist air from the Gulf of Mexico may cause thunderstorms. The western portion of this region is affected by strong, dry winds that blow over the mountains, called *Chinook*. Severe droughts are a major problem in the area. During the droughts, sandstorms often occur. The region is covered with steppe grasses, shrubs, and sagebrush.

The Rocky Mountains stretch from Canada through Idaho, Montana, Wyoming, Utah, Colorado, and New Mexico. The crests of the mountains form the *Continental Divide*. The Continental Divide separates the river systems of the United States into those that flow eastward to the Atlantic and Gulf of Mexico and those that flow westward to the Pacific and the Gulf of California. The Rockies are characterized by rugged, snowcapped mountains. Numerous peaks reach a height of 12,000 feet (3,659 meters). The Rocky Mountains are actually several mountain ranges separated by passes and wide valleys called *parks*. Some of the ranges include Front in Colorado, Teton in Wyoming, Wasatch in Utah, and Sawtooth in Idaho.

Climate in this region varies according to elevation. Desert and grasslands are found at the foot of the mountains. The slopes of the mountains are generally forested. The forests capture the winter snows and help to form the source of rivers that flow down across the Great Plains and the Intermountain Region. The highest mountains reach above the *tree line*. The tree line is the elevation beyond which trees cannot grow.

The Intermountain Region lies between the Rocky Mountains and the Sierra Nevada and Cascade Mountain Ranges. It is a region known for wide open spaces. This region includes most of Arizona, Utah, and Nevada; western Colorado and New Mexico; southern Idaho; and eastern California, Oregon, and Washington. The region consists of rugged mountains, high plateaus, desert basins, and deep canyons. There are actually three sections within this region—the Great Basin, the Colorado Plateau, and the Columbia Plateau.

The Basin Region or the Great Basin is centered in Nevada and extends into Arizona, New Mexico, and California. It is a region of desert basins separated by faulted mountains. A *basin* is a low area of land generally surrounded by mountains. Faulted mountains are the mountains that have risen because of the movement of a fault, a break in the earth's surface. Land on one side of the fault may rise much higher than land on the other side, forming a range of fault-block mountains.

The Colorado Plateau consists of uplifted horizontal rock layers that have been eroded by the wind and water. A *plateau* is a flat-topped tableland that rises above surrounding plains. This region is characterized by deep canyons, including the Grand Canyon of the Colorado River. The Colorado Plateau extends through Colorado, Utah, Arizona, and New Mexico. It rises to an elevation of 10,000 feet (3,048 meters). One feature of this region is known as *Four Corners*. The corners of Utah, Arizona, Colorado, and New Mexico all meet at one point.

The Columbia Plateau begins in southern Utah and extends to eastern Washington and Oregon. It was formed thousands of years ago, when lava flowed through cracks in the earth. The Snake and Columbia Rivers have cut deep canyons into the region.

The climate of the Intermountain Region is varied, depending on the elevation and latitude. In the southern parts, Arizona, New Mexico, and Nevada, the climate is generally continental desert. In the northern parts, Utah and Idaho, it is mainly *continental steppe*. Some of the lowest areas receive almost no rain because they are in a *rain shadow*. A rain shadow is a desert caused by its location on the leeward side of high mountains. Pacific storms are blocked from bringing moisture to the area because of the high Sierra Nevada and Cascade Mountain Ranges.

Student Activities

Part I. Answer each of the following questions.

1. The Rocky Mountain States can really be divided into three large physical regions called _____, _____, and _____.

2. The strong, dry winds that blow over the Rocky Mountains and affect the temperature on the Great Plains are called the _____.

3. The crests of the Rocky Mountains form the _____.

4. What is a *tree line*? _____

_____

5. The Intermountain Region can be divided into three smaller regions called

_____, _____, and _____.

Physical Features of the Rocky Mountain States

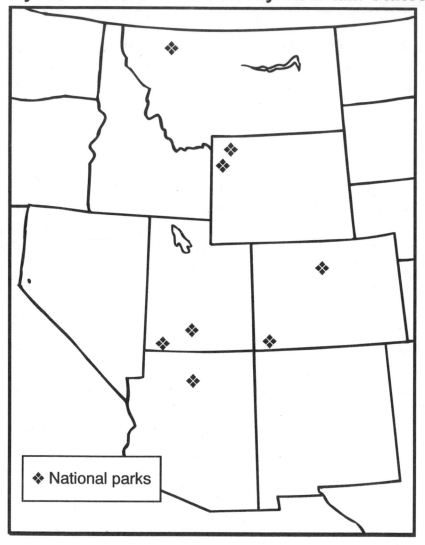

❖ National parks

Part II.

1. On the map above, draw and label the following physical features of the Rocky Mountain States: Great Basin, Sawtooth Mountains, Grand Teton Mountains, Colorado Plateau, Sonora Desert, Columbia Plateau, Great Plains, Front Mountain Range, Wasatch Mountains, Great Salt Lake, Colorado River, Missouri River, North Platte River, South Platte River, Rio Grande River, and Rocky Mountains.

2. Several major national parks are located in the Rocky Mountain States. They have been made national parks because of their outstanding physical features. Label each of the following parks: Carlsbad Caverns, Grand Canyon, Mesa Verde, Bryce Canyon, Zion, Grand Teton, Yellowstone, Waterton-Glacier International Peace, and Rocky Mountain.

Agriculture in the Rocky Mountain States

The lack of moisture is the problem facing agriculture in the Rocky Mountain States. In the Great Plains, for many years the grasslands were considered better suited for grazing than for raising crops. Today, raising livestock is still a major economic activity, but it is often combined with growing wheat. The 100th meridian crosses the Great Plains. To the west of the line, the climate is drier with less than 20 inches (50 centimeters) of rainfall per year. *Irrigation* is necessary for farming. To the east, there is more rain and less chance of crop failure.

Farmers in the western part of the Great Plains have been depending on the Ogallala aquifer for much of their water. An *aquifer* is a rock layer composed mostly of sand and gravel materials through which groundwater can flow. The Ogallala aquifer is a huge underground water storage system that extends from South Dakota to Texas. Unfortunately, the system was being overused and the water level began to drop during the 1950s. The rate of decline has been slowed today.

A number of rivers also cross the Great Plains, including the Missouri, Yellowstone, Platte, Arkansas, and Pecos. These rivers are usually full in the spring but can drop off to only a trickle during the summer. Dams have been built to help control the use of the water so that irrigation needs can be met.

A productive irrigated farm area lies just east of the Rocky Mountains in Colorado and is called the Colorado Piedmont. This area raises sugar beets, corn, beans, and cattle feed. Large beef cattle ranches are found in the Wyoming Basin.

In the Intermountain Region, irrigation is also vital to the production of crops. Cotton and vegetables are the most important irrigated crops in this region. Arizona is a producer of both cotton and vegetables. Sugar beets and wheat are grown in the Salt Lake Basin of Utah. In the northern parts of the region, wheat can be grown without irrigation in Idaho. Idaho is also the leading potato-producing state. It also produces hay for the cattle industry.

Agriculture is possible in the drier areas of this region only because of the Colorado River Basin Projects. For example, the Central Arizona Project carries water from the Colorado River to the cities of Phoenix and Tucson. Dams such as Hoover and Glen Canyon help to provide water for irrigation and hydroelectricity.

The Rio Grande River is also used for irrigation and the production of electricity. Dams help to feed water to the San Luis Valley region of Colorado, the center of New Mexico, and the El Paso, Texas, area. Without these rivers, little farming could be done in the Intermountain Region.

Student Activities

Part I. Answer the following questions.

1. The major problem facing agriculture in the Great Plains and Intermountain Regions of the Rocky Mountain States is the lack of _____.

2. The major agricultural activities in the Great Plains is a combination of _____ and growing _____.

3. The _____ is a large underground water source used in the Great Plains to irrigate the crops.

4. Major rivers that help provide irrigation for the Great Plains include _____, _____, _____, _____, and _____.

5. The irrigated farm region in Colorado east of the Rocky Mountains is called the _____.

6. In the Intermountain Region, _____ and _____ are the two leading irrigated crops.

7. Idaho is the leading producer of _____ in the United States.

8. The Central Arizona Project (CAP) drains water from the _____ River and carries it to the cities of _____ and _____.

9. Irrigation projects in the San Luis Valley of Colorado, central New Mexico, and El Paso, Texas, secure water from the _____ River.

10. The Salt Lake Basin in Utah is the producer of _____ and _____.

Part II. Complete the following activities.

1. Irrigation is vital to the production of agricultural products in the Rocky Mountain States. Various methods of irrigation are used today, including flooding an entire field, channeling water between rows, spraying water through large sprinklers, or letting the water drip onto plants through holes in pipes. Use reference books to find additional information about irrigation methods. Design a poster that shows the various methods used.

2. The amount of irrigated land in the world has doubled in recent years. It is estimated today that 18 percent of all cropland is being irrigated. Work in a small group to list on chart paper some of the problems that this might cause. After the problems are listed, give some possible solutions.

Urban Areas of the Rocky Mountain States

Phoenix is the capital and largest city in Arizona. It is among the ten largest cities in the United States. Phoenix is a manufacturing center and a winter resort area. It is located in the broad, flat Salt River Valley, a region surrounded by low mountains. The Salt River flows westward to become part of the Gila River. Both the Salt and Gila are usually dry in the Phoenix area because they are dammed for irrigation east of the city. Since 1986, water for Phoenix has come from the Central Arizona Project, which brings water from the Colorado River.

The city has a warm, dry climate. The winter temperatures may reach 70° F (21° C). On the average the city has about 300 days of sunny weather each year. The climate has attracted many people to the area.

Phoenix was first occupied by the Hohokim Indians who used irrigation to water their crops. The Spanish then came into the area. In the 1860s the first white settlers moved to the area. Two of those settlers were Jack Swilling and Darrel Duppa. They realized that the town was being built on the site of an ancient settlement. They predicted that a great city would rise in the valley and suggested the name Phoenix. The phoenix is a mythical bird connected with Greek and Egyptian mythology. After a lifespan of 500 years, it would burn itself and a new phoenix would arise from the ashes. This new city would rise from the ruins of an ancient village.

The city of Phoenix has grown to become one of the ten largest cities in the United States. Today, the city covers 450 square miles (1,165 square kilometers). The major industries include aircraft, aircraft engines and parts, computers, guidance and navigational equipment, and semiconductors. In addition, tourism is a major business for Phoenix. Visitors come to the city particularly during the winter. Golf courses and vacation resorts are important to the economy.

Denver is the largest city in the Great Plains region. It is located on the South Platte River about 10 miles (16 kilometers) from the Rocky Mountains. It is nicknamed the "Mile High City" because the state capitol stands on land one mile (1.6 kilometers) above sea level. The city covers 114 square miles (295 square kilometers) and has the same boundaries as Denver County. Denver and nearby Boulder form a consolidated metropolitan area that covers 4,528 square miles (11,727 square kilometers).

Denver was founded in 1858, after the discovery of gold at Cherry Creek. Named for James W. Denver, the governor of the Kansas Territory, the community became a supply center for the Pikes Peak gold rush of 1859. Denver was incorporated in 1861. It became the capital of the Colorado Territory in 1867 and the capital of Colorado when it became a state in 1876.

Today, Denver is an important manufacturing and distributing center. Food processing ranks as the leading manufacturing activity. Other products include defense, high-technology, and transportation equipment. There are so many federal government offices in the city that it is sometimes called the "Washington of the West." A mint located near the city makes millions of U.S. coins every year.

Salt Lake City is the capital and largest city in Utah. It is the world headquarters of the Church of Jesus Christ of Latter-day Saints, commonly known as the Mormons. Over half of the people living in the city are Mormon. Salt Lake City has become a chief center of culture, industry, finance, and transportation in the Rocky Mountains.

The city is located in Salt Lake Valley in the Wasatch Range of the Rocky Mountains. It is located 15 miles (24 kilometers) south of the Great Salt Lake. The city was founded on July 24, 1847, by Mormons who were escaping persecution in Illinois. It was named after the Great Salt Lake. Brigham Young, leader of the Mormons, chose the spot which he had seen in a vision. The Mormon Temple stands on Temple Square in the heart of the city. The city occupies 75 square miles (194 square kilometers) and is the county seat of Salt Lake County.

Salt Lake City has developed into an industrial center. Its major industries include aircraft parts, chemicals, computer software, electronics, and food products. Some petroleum refineries are also located in the area. Much of the industrial importance is based on the rich natural resources of the area. These resources include copper, chlorides, magnesium, and potash.

These three cities, one from each of the three major physical regions of the Rocky Mountain States, are representative of the urban development that is taking place in this area. Many problems that go along with urban growth remain in this region. The limited amount of water is being further strained by urban development. Cities such as Phoenix and Denver have major air pollution problems. Some cities have grown rapidly without adequate traffic management or housing. Future changes should incorporate preservation of the environment as well as economic development.

Student Activities

Part I. Fill in the blanks with the correct answers based on the clues given below.

_____ 1. capital and largest city in Arizona

_____ 2. leader of the Mormons who chose Salt Lake Valley for their home

_____ 3. Native-American tribe that had an ancient village in the Salt River Valley

_____ 4. nicknamed the "Mile High City" because the capitol building is one mile above sea level

_____ 5. city named for a mythical bird that rose out of the ashes every 500 years

_____ 6. common name given to the Church of Jesus Christ of Latter-Day Saints

_____ 7. city with the nickname "Washington of the West" because of the number of federal government offices located there

_____ 8. aqueduct project that brings water from the Colorado River to the city of Phoenix

_____ 9. because of the weather, tourism has become a major business in this city with golf courses and vacation resorts

_____ 10. natural resources near this city include copper, chlorides, magnesium, and potash

Part II. Complete the following activities.

1. Urban development in the Rocky Mountain States can lead to problems. In small groups, list on chart paper potential problems that might be caused by growth. Then design a model city for the future that would try to solve these problems. Make a map of your city showing each part and how it would be constructed. As you work on the city, keep in mind all of the various services that you will need to provide. Share your model city with the class.

2. Organize the information given in this selection on a chart comparing the three cities studied. Decide what topics you want to compare about each city. Use those topics as the headings in your chart. Include at least five topics in your comparison. Share your chart with others in the class.

Native Americans in the Rocky Mountain States

The first inhabitants of the Intermountain Region were the Native Americans, who arrived about 12,000 years ago. The first major agricultural society was started around A.D. 600. When the Spanish arrived in the fourteenth century, there were 100,000 Native Americans living in this region. Most of the tribes were farmers, but there were some nomadic hunters such as the Apaches and Utes.

The Apache Indians belong to one of five tribes in the southwestern United States. Today, approximately 16,000 live on reservations in Arizona and New Mexico. The Apache gained a reputation for being warlike because of their resistance to being placed on reservations by the U.S. Government.

The Apaches were hunters who tracked game and gathered wild plants for food. They often lived in *tepees* made of skins as they followed their game. They resisted when the government wanted to put them on reservations. However, they were defeated by the U.S. Army and forced onto the reservations in the 1870s. In 1885, Geronimo led a rebellion. He was tracked and forced to surrender the following year.

Today, the Apache Tribe owns lumber and cattle companies. Many of the tribe members work at these companies. The Jicarilla Apache also earn income from the mineral rights on their reservations. In 1982, the Supreme Court upheld their right to tax the production of oil and natural gas on their lands.

There are about 7,000 Ute Indians living on three reservations in Utah and Colorado. The Utes were also hunters who built cone-shaped houses out of brush or lived in tepees. They assigned hunting grounds to families who hunted the buffalo, elk, and antelope. Once a year they would travel to New Mexico to trade with the Pueblo Indians and with Spaniards. During the 1600s they got horses from the Spaniards; this increased their mobility. They developed an economy based on trading meat and hides for other goods. Today, many members of the tribe work in agriculture, forestry, and tourism.

The best-known chief of the Ute was Ouray. He spoke Spanish, English, and several Native-American languages. He helped to settle disputes between the Ute and early settlers and arranged the first treaty between the Ute and the United States Government. The Ute were assigned to reservations in the late 1800s.

The largest Native-American population today lives on the Colorado Plateau of Arizona and New Mexico. The Navajo and Hopi are the largest nations. The Navajo are the second largest nation in the United States after the Cherokee Nation. The Navajo reservation covers about 16 million acres (6.5 million hectares) in Arizona, New Mexico, and Utah. The Navajo refer to themselves as *Deni*, which means "the people."

About 150,000 Navajo live on the reservation. Some still live in *hogans*, the traditional tribal houses made of logs and earth. Traditionally, the Navajos were nomadic herders of sheep, goats, and horses, moving in search of pasture lands. But now many are farmers, teachers, miners, engineers, or technicians. The tribe owns a lumber mill and a manufacturing plant, in addition to mining its vast coal deposits. The Navajo are known for their artistic skills in making baskets, blankets, and jewelry.

The Navajo began to raise sheep in the 1600s. When white settlers began to establish ranches on Navajo land, the tribe fought to drive them off. In 1864, U.S. Army troops led by Kit Carson defeated the Navajo, destroying their farms and houses. About 8,000 were forced to march more than 300 miles (480 kilometers) to Fort Sumner, New Mexico, in what is now called the "Long Walk." Thousands died during the march and during their imprisonment at the fort. In 1868, the tribe settled on the reservation.

About 3,500 Hopi, one of the Pueblo Indian tribes, live on the reservations in northeastern Arizona. There are 11 villages on or near three high *mesas*. A mesa is a broad, flat-topped landform with steep sides. One of the villages, Oraibi, was founded 800 years ago and is one of the oldest continuously inhabited villages in the United States.

The Hopi are known for being farmers and craft workers. They grow crops on valley lands and graze sheep and goats on surrounding lands. Additional income comes from making and selling baskets, pottery, silver jewelry, and *kachina dolls*. These carved wooden dolls represent messengers from the gods.

Student Activities

Part I. Using the following clues, identify the Native-American group that is being described.

_____ 1. Geronimo led a rebellion but was defeated by the U.S. Army.

_____ 2. built cone-shaped houses out of brush as they hunted their game

_____ 3. one of the Pueblo Indian tribes now living in northeastern Arizona

_____ 4. the second largest Native-American nation in the United States

_____ 5. forced by U.S. Troops to make the "Long Walk" of more than 300 miles (480 kilometers) to Fort Sumner, New Mexico

_____ 6. the village, Oraibi, is one of the oldest continuously inhabited villages in the United States

_____ 7. developed an economy based on trading meat and hides for other goods

_____ 8. the Supreme Court recently gave this tribe the right to tax the oil and natural gas produced on its lands

_____ 9. their villages are located on or near mesas in northeastern Arizona

_____ 10. This tribe owns vast coal deposits, a lumber mill, and a manufacturing plant.

Part II. Complete the following activities.

1. There have been many great leaders among the Native Americans. Two of these leaders, Geronimo (Apache) and Ouray (Ute), were mentioned in this study. Others could include Cochise (Chiricahua Apache), Chief Joseph (Nez Perce), Red Cloud (Oglala Sioux), Sacagawea (Shoshone), and Wovoka (Paiute). Choose one of these leaders or another of your choice to research. Find out as much information as possible about each person and what he or she did that made this person a great leader. Role-play that you are that leader and write a first-person paper telling about your life. Tell your story to the rest of the class.

2. Choose one of the Native American tribes living in the Rocky Mountain States to research. Find out about the tribe's life before the coming of the white settlers and compare it to life after the coming of the settlers. Create two collages on poster board showing the tribes as they were before the settlement of the West and as they are now. Included on the collages should be types of houses, jobs, traditions, a map showing where the tribe lived, and other information that you are able to find. Share your collages with the entire class.

The Pacific States

Goals for This Unit

Students will

1. use relative and absolute location clues to locate sites in the Pacific States.
2. label the major physical regions of the Pacific States.
3. compare and contrast major urban areas located in the Pacific States.
4. map the Oregon Trail and summarize the hardships encountered by settlers moving west to begin a new life for their families.

Rationale

The Pacific States covered in this unit will include California, Oregon, and Washington. These three states are the westernmost states of the contiguous United States. These states themselves are sometimes divided into the two regions of California and the Pacific Northwest. This area is noted for its agricultural production, forest products, and major urban centers (especially in California). Los Angeles is the second largest metropolitan area in the United States and is world famous for the film and television industry that is centered there. This region is one of contrasts that provides the opportunity to study both the advantages and the problems that come with rapid growth.

Skills Taught in This Unit

brainstorming	collage making	map labeling
graphing	organizing time lines	creating Venn diagrams
comparing/contrasting	charting	booklet making

Vocabulary

presidio	contiguous	fault
caldera		

Background Material

The activities in this unit will provide a glimpse of California, Oregon, and Washington. Students will use the five themes of geography to analyze and chart the similarities and differences found in these three states. Dramatic differences will be noted as they find that California is the most urbanized state in the United States. The other two states are much more rural. Southern California has large cities that are facing the problem of water shortages. These cities must find ways to increase the amount of available water as their populations increase. These differences, and similarities, will involve students in analyzing potential problems facing this region in the future.

Location in the Pacific States

The Pacific States on the mainland of the United States include California, Oregon, and Washington. Alaska and Hawaii are also Pacific States but will be considered in a separate section. This activity will involve students in using absolute and relative location to correctly identify sites in these three states. The intent of this activity is to provide practice in the use of absolute and relative location as tools of geography. These tools help identify the location of any place in the world.

Objectives

Students will
1. use relative and absolute location clues to locate sites in the Pacific States.
2. label and color a map of the Pacific States.

Materials: "Location in the Pacific States" student activity sheets, atlases, textbooks, color pencils, pencils

Procedure
1. Locate in class the three states of the contiguous 48 states that are bordered by the Pacific Ocean. Explain that there are actually five states but that the other two are great distances away from these three. They will be studied separately.
2. Review the terms *absolute* and *relative location*. Give an example of each type of location.
3. Students should use the classroom atlases, reference books, or their textbooks to complete the activities on the student sheets. Remind students that all labeling of maps should be done in manuscript and that any coloring should be done with colored pencils.
4. Display some of the better maps in class.

Physical Features of the Pacific States

The Pacific States are really composed of three mountain ranges and the valleys that separate the ranges. Those three ranges are the Coast Ranges, the Sierra Nevada Range, and the Cascade Range. Each range is made up of several smaller mountain ranges. The Coast Ranges form the rugged mountainous coast along much of the three states. This range includes the Olympic Mountains in Washington and the Klamath Mountains in Oregon. The Cascade Range begins with Mount Baker in northern Washington and extends to Mount Lassen in northern California. Included in this range are many volcanic mountains, including Mount St. Helens. The Sierra Nevada Range contains very tall mountains and includes Mount Whitney, the highest peak in the contiguous United States. Between these ranges are fertile valleys that are important for agriculture. In the southern region of California, the Mojave Desert is part of the basin and range region. Included in this region is Death Valley, the lowest point in North America.

Objectives
Students will
1. read about the major physical regions of the Pacific States.
2. identify major physical regions on a map.

Materials: "Physical Regions of the Pacific States" student activity sheets, colored pencils, pencils, reference books, atlases

Procedure
1. Use a physical wall map or overhead map to locate the Pacific States. By looking at the map, ask students to identify some of the physical features they notice in the three states. List these features on the board.
2. Read the "Physical Features of the Pacific States" student activity sheets. Ask students to identify additional physical features that could be added to the list.
3. Assign the seven questions in Part I to serve as a review of the material just read. Go over the questions in class.
4. Assign each student the map activity in Part II. Remind students that all labeling should be clearly printed and that all coloring should be done with colored pencils. Classroom atlases and other reference books will be needed to complete this activity.

Urban Areas of the Pacific States
Themes of Geography: Human-Environment Interaction, Region

California is the most urbanized state in the United States. It contains the second largest metropolitan area in the country, Los Angeles. Other major metropolitan areas include San Francisco, San Diego, Seattle, and Portland. The urban areas have become major centers of commerce and industry for their states. This activity will give students a brief glimpse of the five largest cities in the Pacific States and some of the individual characteristics of each.

Objectives
Students will
1. identify urban areas based on clues giving facts about each city.
2. complete a chart comparing the five cities.
3. prepare a booklet on a chosen city.
4. complete a Venn Diagram showing similarities and differences between two cities.

Materials: "Urban Areas of the Pacific States" student activity sheets, reference books, paper, pencils, crayons, colored pencils, paper for use in making a booklet, chart paper

Procedure
1. Ask students to identify major urban areas with which they are familiar in the Pacific States. Then, list on chart paper any facts they know about the five cities covered in this study. Put this paper on the wall for future reference.

2. Read "Urban Areas of the Pacific States" student activity sheets. Discuss facts given about the five cities. Compare this information with the information placed on the chart paper earlier. Make corrections and additions as needed.
3. Assign Part I to be completed by students. Go over this material as a review.
4. In the first activity in Part II, students should summarize the information from the student activity sheets by filling in the columns of the chart.
5. The making of a booklet on one of the cities will require the use of reference books and textbooks. Explain how the books are to be made and what topics are to be included. Let the class discuss what a finished booklet should look like. Create a rubric to use in grading the booklets.
6. Discuss with the class the concept of the Venn Diagram. Explain that characteristics that are true of both cities would be placed in the overlapping part of the two circles. Characteristics true of only one city would be placed in the circle under that city's name. Give students time to share their diagrams.

The Oregon Trail

Themes of Geography: Movement, Region

Several trails were established throughout the West to allow settlers to move into the new lands. The Oregon Trail is the longest and one of the best-known trails. The story of this trail is one of danger, misfortune, hope, and new beginnings. Although thousands were killed in making the journey, nearly 12,000 settlers had moved into the Willamette Valley to make a new beginning in life by the time the Oregon Territory was created. These early settlers braved the hardships and dangers of this trail so that they and their families might have a better life. This activity will highlight the route of the Oregon Trail and some of the hardships that awaited the settlers.

Objectives
Students will
1. label and trace the route followed by the Oregon Trail.
2. complete a time line of major events related to the Oregon Trail.
3. discuss some of the hardships endured by the settlers as they tried to gain a better life for their families.

Materials: "The Oregon Trail" student activity sheets, paper, pencil, atlases, reference books, chart paper

Procedure
1. Divide your class into groups of five. Give the following setting for the assignment. The year is 1843. Your family has decided to move to Oregon from Independence, Missouri. The trail that you will be following is nearly 2,000 miles (3,200 kilometers) in length. You can take only what you can fit into a covered wagon. Discuss in your group, and make a list on chart paper, the items you would need to take on your trip. Allow each group to share with the class.

2. Read "The Oregon Trail" student activity sheets. Discuss the hardships that were encountered along the trail. Now that students are aware of some of the hardships of the trip, ask if they would change any of the materials they decided to take with them.
3. Students should use reference books and atlases to complete the map activity of labeling each site and drawing in the Oregon Trail. Remind students that all labeling of maps should be done in manuscript.
4. Students should complete the time line of events related to the Oregon Trail.
5. Discuss how trails such as the Oregon Trail assisted with the settlement of the Pacific States.

Conclusion

This unit has provided a look at the three contiguous Pacific States. While different in many ways, they share a similar history and face many common problems in the future. These states are vital to the economy of the United States because of the varied resources and manufactured products they provide. This study has given students a glimpse into the cultural geography of the area. This information will help to further students' understanding of the varied cultures of the United States.

Location in the Pacific States

The three states of California, Oregon, and Washington form the Pacific States of the mainland United States. This region is sometimes subdivided into California and the Pacific Northwest. California contains about 12 percent of the United States' population.

Standing alone, the economy of California would rank number six in the world. Washington and Oregon are producers of fishing, farming, and forestry products. The other two Pacific States, Alaska and Hawaii, will be considered separately.

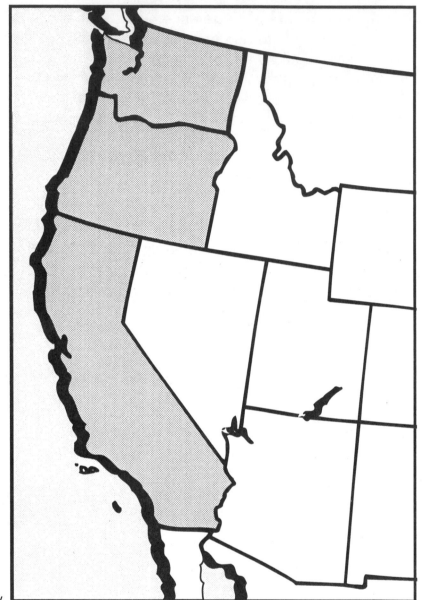

1. These states are bordered by three Rocky Mountain States. Name those states and then label them on the map:

   a. _____ b. _____ c. _____

2. _____ is the foreign country that borders California to the south. Label this country on the map.

3. _____ is the foreign country that borders Washington to the north. Label this country on the map.

4. Identify the following cities and label them on the map.

_____ a. This capital city is located on the Willamette River at 44° 55' N and 123° 3' W.

_____ b. This California city located at 37° 45' N and 122° 26' W is located beside a bay that bears the same name.

_____ c. This capital city is located near the Sacramento River at 38° 35' N and 121° 30' W.

_____ d. This capital city is located at the far southern point of the Puget Sound at 47° 2' N and 122° 52' W.

_____ e. This city is located on the Spokane River in eastern Washington near the border of Idaho.

_____ f. This southern California city is located just north of the city of Tijuana, Mexico.

_____ g. The largest city in Washington, located at 47° 36' N and 122° 20' W, is on the east shore of Puget Sound.

_____ h. The second largest city in the United States is located at 34° N and 118° 15' W on the southwestern shore of California.

_____ i. The third largest city in Washington is located on Puget Sound between Olympia and Seattle.

_____ j. The largest city in Oregon is located near the Columbia River just south of Washington.

5. Identify each of the states below by using the relative location clues. Then label each state on the map.

_____ a. is located north of Mexico, west of Arizona and Nevada, south of Oregon, and east of the Pacific Ocean.

_____ b. is located south of British Columbia, west of Idaho, north of Oregon, and east of the Pacific Ocean.

_____ c. is located north of California and Nevada, west of Idaho, south of Washington, and east of the Pacific Ocean.

Physical Features of the Pacific States

The Pacific States are made up of three major mountain ranges and the valleys that separate them. The three ranges include the Coast Ranges, the Cascade Range, and the Sierra Nevada Range.

The Coast Ranges extend from Canada to Mexico. They are really a series of parallel mountain ranges. In most of the region they form a rugged coastline; however, there are a few lowland areas between the mountains and the sea. The largest lowland area is the Los Angeles Basin. The Coast Ranges also form the eight Channel Islands off the coast of southern California. There are two mountain ranges in this region. The Olympic Mountains are located in the Olympic Peninsula in northwestern Washington. These mountains are glaciated. The other range is the forested Klamath Mountains in the southwestern corner of Oregon.

East of the Coast Ranges are the Sierra Nevada and Cascade Ranges. The Sierra Nevada Range is located in the eastern region of California. This range of faulted and glaciated mountains is one of the longest and highest ranges in the United States. Mount Whitney, with an elevation of 14,494 feet (4,419 meters), is the highest mountain in the *contiguous* states. (Contiguous states are the 48 states that are located side by side in the mainland of the United States.) This region is dotted with hundreds of lakes, including Lake Tahoe.

South of the Sierra Nevada Range lies the basin and range region of Southern California. This area extends to the Colorado River and includes the Mojave Desert. Death Valley is in this region near the Nevada border. Part of Death Valley lies 282 feet (86 meters) below sea level and is the lowest point in North America.

The Cascade Range runs from Mount Baker in northern Washington to Mount Lassen in northern California. These mountains are volcanic. The largest of the volcanoes are Mount Rainier, Mount Hood, and Mount Shasta. These mountains also include the active volcano, Mount St. Helens, in Washington and Crater Lake in Oregon. Crater Lake is the deepest lake in the United States. At the deepest point, the lake is 1,932 feet (589 meters). The lake is situated in the *caldera* of Mount Mazama. A caldera is the depression in the earth formed after a volcano erupts or collapses.

Between these mountain ranges are lowlands that include three major valleys. The Puget Sound Lowlands are located just east of the Puget Sound in the northwest corner of Washington. The Willamette Valley lies along the Willamette River in the northwestern area of Oregon. The Central Valley lies between the Coast Ranges and the Sierra Nevada Mountains in California. All three valleys are fertile and important agricultural areas.

The Pacific States, especially California, frequently experience earthquakes. The Pacific Plate is moving northward along the San Andreas *Fault*. A fault is the result of rock layers that break and move apart. In this case, the San Andreas Fault is the line along which the Pacific Plate meets the North American Plate. As the Pacific Plate continues to move, pressure builds up between the plates. The movement of rocks along the fault will cause shock waves that create earthquakes. Scientists are warning that Washington and Oregon could also experience earthquakes because of an active fault line off their coast.

Student Activities

Part I. Complete each of the following statements.

1. The Pacific States of the United States can be divided into the following three mountain ranges: _____, _____, and _____.

2. _____ is the tallest mountain located in the 48 contiguous United States.

3. _____, located in the caldera of Mount Mazama, is the deepest lake in the United States.

4. _____, located in the basin and range region of southern California, is the lowest point in North America.

5. A _____ is the line along which two plates of the earth's surface meet. There is a break in the rock layers.

6. The _____ Fault marks the line along which the Pacific Plate rubs against the North American Plate.

7. The three valleys that are fertile and centers of agricultural production are _____, _____, and _____.

Part II. Complete the following map activity.

1. On the map on the following page, locate and label each of the following sites:
   Mountains: Coast Ranges, Sierra Nevada Range, Cascade Range, Mount Rainier, Mount St. Helens, Mount Lassen, Mount Shasta, Mount Whitney, Mount Baker

Valleys (Lowlands): Puget Sound Lowlands, Willamette Valley, Central Valley, Death Valley

Lakes: Lake Tahoe, Crater Lake

Bays and Sounds: San Francisco Bay, Puget Sound

2. Color the Pacific Ocean light blue and label it on the map.

3. Label the three Pacific States and use a colored pencil to color them light brown.

The Pacific States

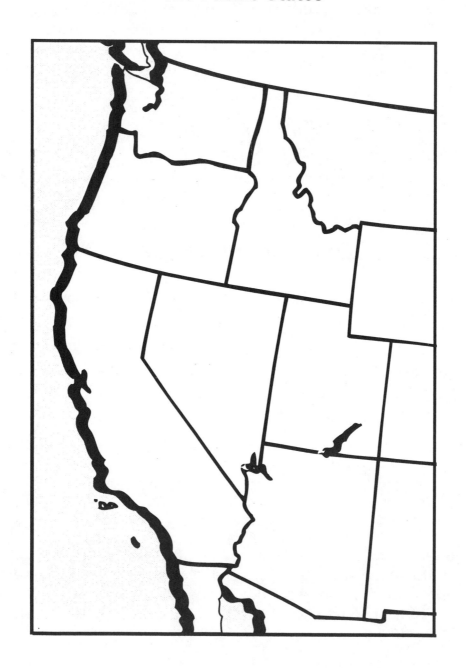

Urban Areas of the Pacific States

California is the most urbanized state in the United States. More than 90 percent of its population lives in urban areas. The three largest areas are the Los Angeles Basin, San Francisco, and San Diego County. In the Pacific Northwest, the two major cities are Seattle, Washington, and Portland, Oregon.

Los Angeles began as a small town but has grown to become a huge city in southern California. The Pueblo of Los Angeles was first started in 1781 by settlers from Mexico. It had a population of 44 persons. Today, the metropolitan area of Los Angeles is the second largest city in the United States. The city is home to about 3.5 million people. The metropolitan area is made up of 84 cities and has a population of about nine million people.

Los Angeles is the financial, industrial, and trade center of the western United States. It is a large manufacturing center, producing more aircraft and space exploration equipment than any other city in the United States. In addition, the movie and television industry located here has gained worldwide attention. The Port of Los Angeles is one of the busiest on the West Coast. Thousands of ships arrive at the port each year.

Los Angeles covers 466 square miles (1,207 square kilometers). It stretches about 50 miles (80 kilometers) from the San Fernando Valley in the north to the Los Angeles Harbor at San Pedro Bay in the south. The city covers about 30 miles (48 kilometers) east to west from the San Gabriel Mountains to the Pacific Ocean. Tourism is an important business in Los Angeles. Millions of tourists come to the city each year to enjoy the recreational facilities as well as the cultural and entertainment attractions.

The rapid growth of population in Los Angeles has caused problems that must be solved. The city has little open space left and housing is in short supply. There are also over five million cars on the highways of the city. Freeways are often crowded, and exhaust fumes have caused a major air pollution problem. In response to these problems, the city has improved its bus system and is currently building a subway. A light rail train system is also under construction.

San Francisco, with a population of over 700,000 people, is the second largest city in California. The city is known as a cultural, financial, and industrial center. The city was founded in 1776 by Spanish settlers. Gold was discovered east of the city in 1848 and the city became a major mining supply center. In 1906, an earthquake and fire destroyed most of the city.

Today, San Francisco has one of the largest Asian populations on the mainland United States. About 200,000 people of Asian ancestry live in the city. About 82,000 of this number are Chinese or of Chinese ancestry. Many of the first Chinese came over to work on the Transcontinental Railroad. San Francisco's Chinatown helps to draw many tourists to the city.

The city is built on or around more than 40 hills. Some of the steepest streets in the world lie in the downtown area of San Francisco. These hills rise as much as 376 feet (115 meters). San Francisco covers 129 square miles (334 square kilometers) including 83 square miles (215 square kilometers) of water. Included in this area are several islands in the San Francisco Bay and the Pacific Ocean. Alcatraz is probably the most famous of the islands. It was once a federal prison.

San Diego is a naval and aerospace center. The city includes a natural deepwater harbor. The harbor is home to oceangoing ships, tuna fleets, and United States Naval vessels. The city is one of the fastest-growing cities in the United States. It is also one of the oldest cities in California and is sometimes called "the Birthplace of California." It was founded in 1769, when California's first *presidio* (military fort) was built by the Spanish. That same year, Junípero Serra, a Franciscan priest, established the first mission in the presidio. The city covers 360 square miles (930 square kilometers), including 70 square miles (181 square kilometers) of inland water.

Seattle serves as a manufacturing, trade, and transportation center for the Pacific Northwest. The city covers 86 square miles (223 square kilometers) located on the east shore of Puget Sound. The city was founded in 1852 by settlers from Illinois. The lumber industry helped the city to grow. Lumber from surrounding forests was brought to Seattle for shipment to markets around the world. Seattle is also a center for aircraft and spacecraft manufacturing.

Portland is Oregon's largest city and a major center for industry and trade. The city was founded in 1845 by two New England land developers, Asa Lovejoy of Boston and Francis Pettygrove of Portland, Maine. Located near the junction of the Columbia and Willamette Rivers, the city is an important West Coast port. About 45 percent of Oregon's total population is in the Portland Metropolitan Area. The city covers about 112 square miles (290 square kilometers), including six square miles (15 square kilometers) of inland water. Industries in the area include computer and electronic equipment, food products, lumber and wood products, and textiles.

Student Activities

Part I. Answer the following questions by filling in the blanks with the name of the appropriate urban areas.

_____ 1. The metropolitan area of this city is the second largest in the United States.

_____ 2. This city, built on or around more than 40 hills, contains some of the steepest streets in the world.

_____ 3. This important West Coast port is located near the junction of the Columbia and Willamette Rivers.

_____ 4. This city was founded in 1852 by settlers coming from Illinois.

_____ 5. This city was founded in 1769 by Spanish soldiers when California's first presidio was built.

_____ 6. This city's metropolitan area contains about 45 percent of the total population of the state.

_____ 7. This city is noted for the movie and television industry as well as being a center for aircraft and space exploration equipment.

_____ 8. This city has one of the largest Asian populations in the United States with 200,000 people of Asian ancestry.

_____ 9. This city is a naval and aerospace center with a large natural deepwater harbor.

_____ 10. This city first began to grow because of the timber industry.

Part II. Complete the following activities.

1. Organize the information in this selection to fit into the following chart.

City	Date Founded	Area	Major Industries

2. Choose one of these five cities as a topic for additional research. Put together a booklet on your city. Include information on the following topics: history, government, economy, education, and cultural events. Include in the booklet a map showing where the city is located. If the city has symbols such as a flag or seal, include drawings of them. Share your book with the rest of the class.

3. Choose two of the cities mentioned in this selection and create a Venn diagram showing similarities and differences. Similarities are written in the area where the two circles overlap.

The Oregon Trail

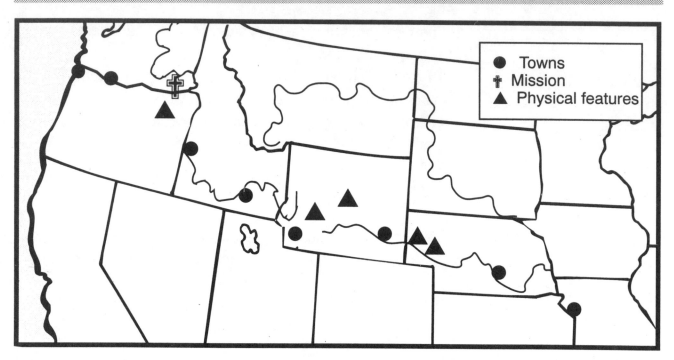

The Oregon Trail was the longest of the overland routes used in the westward expansion of the United States. The trail ran for nearly 2,000 miles from Independence, Missouri, to Oregon. It wound through prairies, deserts, and mountains along the way.

Use the clues below to help trace the route on the map above and correctly label the towns or forts and important physical features found along the trail.

1. Most families left from Independence, Missouri, located in the northwest region of Missouri near the Missouri River. Label Independence, Missouri.
2. Then they traveled northwest into Nebraska to Fort Kearny. Label Fort Kearny.
3. The trail then followed the Platte River past Chimney Rock and Scotts Bluff to Fort Laramie, Wyoming. Label Chimney Rock, Scotts Bluff, and Fort Laramie.
4. From Fort Laramie, they continued along the North Platte River past Independence Rock and through South Pass to Fort Bridger. Label Independence Rock, South Pass, and Fort Bridger.
5. Leaving from Fort Bridger, the trail went to Fort Hall near the Snake River and then on to Fort Boise, Idaho. Label Fort Hall and Fort Boise.
6. Settlers then crossed the Grande Ronde Valley to Marcus Whitman's Mission in Walla Walla, Washington. Label Grande Ronde Valley and Whitman's Mission.
7. From here, they traveled down the Columbia River to Fort Vancouver and the Willamette Valley of Oregon.
8. Draw a line linking each of the sites labeled on the map. This line will represent the Oregon Trail.

The route of the Oregon Trail was first blazed by trappers and explorers. Meriwether Lewis and William Clark traveled on the Snake and Columbia Rivers section of the trail in 1805. Traders returning from Astoria used part of the trail. Benjamin Bonneville took the first wagons through the South Pass in the 1830s. John C. Frémont surveyed a portion of the trail for the United States Army in 1842.

Settlers began using the trail around 1841. The first large group, about 900, used the trail in the "Great Migration" of 1843. In that same year, a provisional government was set up. The northern boundary of the Oregon Country was set in 1846 and the Territory was created in 1848. By the time the Oregon Territory was created by Congress, nearly 12,000 settlers had made the journey over the Oregon Trail.

The wagons of the settlers were often not very sturdy. They were wooden boxes covered with a canopy of oil cloth and set over a frame on iron-rimmed wheels. Wagons were often washed away while trying to cross rivers, and settlers would often drown. The wheels would get stuck in the mud of the trail and the axles could easily break on the rough mountain terrain. Trees and rocks had to be removed from the trail to allow the wagons to pass. In addition to these hardships, the settlers had to reach Oregon before the harsh winter set in. There was also a constant danger from Native Americans angered by the settlers crossing their land.

Disease and harsh climate contributed to the deaths of many settlers on the trail. It is estimated that thousands were buried in shallow graves along the route. The graves were left unmarked so that wild animals and thieves would not be able to detect them. Drivers would run their wagons over the graves to erase the sight of the diggings. In spite of the dangers encountered along the trail, thousands were able to move into the Willamette Valley and help found the state of Oregon.

Student Activities

Part I. Complete the following time line on the Oregon Trail by writing either the date or the event which occurred.

Date	Events
_____	Lewis and Clark traveled on part of the trail.
1830s	_____
1841	_____
_____	John C. Frémont surveyed part of the Oregon Trail.
_____	The "Great Migration" took place—when over 900 used the trail.
1846	_____
_____	Territory of Oregon created.

Part II. Answer the following questions.
1. By the time Oregon was made a territory, nearly _____ settlers had moved across the trail.
2. What are some of the hardships faced by the settlers on the trail?

Alaska and Hawaii

Goals for This Unit

Students will

1. discuss the relative and absolute location of Alaska and Hawaii and label a map showing selected sites.
2. make a map of products from Alaska and Hawaii.
3. write a journal describing the life of a gold prospector in 1890.

Rationale

Alaska and Hawaii are the two states separated from the contiguous United States. Each of these states is very different in location and physical environment. The study of these states shows a great contrast between two regions. However, there are also many common elements that help to bind them to the United States. The study of these states provides students a glimpse of life in these two unique regions.

Skills Taught in This Unit

mapping   writing journals   forming a consensus
role-playing   creating product maps

Vocabulary

panhandle   peninsula   volcanic soil
placer deposits

Background Material

Alaska and Hawaii are two very different regions within the United States. They vary from the largest state in area in the northwestern corner of North America to a chain of volcanic islands in the Pacific near the same latitude as the central parts of Mexico. From a tundra climate to a tropical one, the lifestyles of the people are very different. However, there are common bonds that bind them together and make them a valuable part of the United States.

Location in Alaska

Themes of Geography: Location, Place, Human-Environment Interaction, Movement, Region

Alaska is the largest state in area in the United States. Because of its often harsh climate, it has one of the smallest populations of any state. Alaska is a peninsula on the northwest corner of North America. It has several peninsulas and a panhandle that help to form its distinctive shape. This activity will provide a description of many of the physical features of Alaska and where they are located. It will also show how humans have affected the environment by building the Alaska Pipeline to move oil to the south shore so that it can be shipped out all during the year. Students will be asked to label a map identifying the major physical regions of Alaska.

Objectives

Students will
1. discuss the location and physical features of Alaska.
2. complete a map showing the locations of cities and major physical features of Alaska.
3. explain how the Trans-Alaska Pipeline is an example of human-environment interaction.

Materials: "Location in Alaska" student activity sheets, paper, pencils, colored pencils, chart paper, atlases, reference books

Procedure

1. Using a wall map, locate the state of Alaska and describe its relative location to the contiguous United States.
2. Read "Location in Alaska" student activity sheets and assign students the questions under Part I. Go over the questions as a review with students.
3. Using maps or textbooks, students should complete the map of Alaska, labeling the items listed in Part II.
4. Discuss with students the Trans-Alaska Pipeline as an example of human-environment interaction.

Resources of Alaska

Themes of Geography: Place, Human-Environment Interaction, Movement, Region

The purchase of Alaska in 1867 was referred to as Seward's Folly. However, the resources that have been found there are of far greater value than the original price. From the discovery of gold in 1890 to the completion of the Alaska Pipeline, natural resources have been exported out of Alaska. This activity will help students gain a better understanding of the state of Alaska and the resources found there.

Objectives

Students will
1. read about and discuss the major resources found in Alaska.
2. make a natural resource map of Alaska.

3. write a journal describing life as a prospector in 1890.
4. debate whether or not Alaska was a good purchase in 1867.

Materials: "Resources of Alaska" student activity sheets, paper, pencils, poster board, chart paper, resource books

Procedure
1. Ask students to name products that are found in Alaska. Make a list of these products.
2. Read "Resources of Alaska" student activity sheets and discuss in class. Assign students the ten questions listed in Part I and go over their answers as a review of the material read.
3. Students will need to use resource books and poster board to make the resource map of Alaska. They should design a symbol for each of the resources of Alaska. The symbols will be placed on the map at the approximate site of the resource in the state. The map should be shared with the class.
4. Students should conduct research on the gold rush of 1890 before beginning the second activity in Part II. They need to be aware of the living conditions and climate conditions that were endured by the prospectors. Students should then write a journal describing life as a prospector for gold in 1890.
5. Since the purchase of Alaska was such a heated topic in 1867, students should role-play being members of the Congress and discussing the issue. They need to work in groups to list reasons for purchasing and for not purchasing the new territory. Each group should come to consensus on how members would have voted and state the reasons for their decisions.

Location in Hawaii

Themes of Geography: Location, Place, Region

Hawaii is the only state that is not located on the continent of North America. Its distance from the other states and its tropical climate make Hawaii a fascinating study. This activity will introduce students to both the absolute location and relative location of Hawaii. It will also introduce many of the physical features of the eight major islands. Students will gain an overview of the physical geography of Hawaii.

Objectives
Students will
1. use location and place geography clues to identify the major islands of Hawaii.
2. label a map showing the location of specific sites and major physical features of the islands of Hawaii.

Materials: "Location in Hawaii" student activity sheets, pencils, paper, colored pencils, atlases, reference books

Procedure
1. Locate Hawaii on a wall map. Discuss the relative and absolute location of the islands. Ask students to identify ways Hawaii's location distinguishes it from other states.

2. Read "Location in Hawaii" student activity sheets. After discussing the material read, students should use the clues to identify the major islands described in Part I.
3. Assign students to complete Part II. Go over the questions in class.
4. Students should use atlases and resource books to label the map of Hawaii. Remind students that all labeling should be printed.

Resources of Hawaii

Themes of Geography: Human-Environment Interaction, Movement, Region

The tropical climate and volcanic soil in Hawaii make good growing conditions for the crops of sugar cane and pineapples. The raising of these products, plus cattle ranching, dairy farming, and food processing are some of the industries found in Hawaii. This activity will feature these industries and introduce students to the major products from Hawaii.

Objectives
Students will
1. read and discuss the major resources and products of Hawaii.
2. create a product map of Hawaii.

Materials: "Resources of Hawaii" student activity sheet, paper, pencils, reference books, poster board

Procedure
1. Ask students to identify major products produced in Hawaii. Make a list of these products.
2. Read "Resources of Hawaii" student activity sheet. Discuss the information given describing the major resources and products of Hawaii.
3. Ask students to answer the questions under Part I. Go over the answers as a review of the material.
4. Students will need to use poster board and reference books to make the product maps of Hawaii. An outline map of the major islands should be drawn on the poster board. Then symbols should be drawn representing the major products of the islands. The symbols are then pasted on the map in the appropriate places. The maps should be shared with the class.

Conclusion

The two regions studied in this unit are very different. Hopefully, students will realize that even though the differences in geography are considerable, there are major elements uniting the two regions as part of the United States. Both Alaska and Hawaii have problems that will need to be solved in the future. Some of the problems are the same for both regions as well as other regions of the United States. Hopefully, better understanding of each region will provide better chances of solving these problems.

Location in Alaska

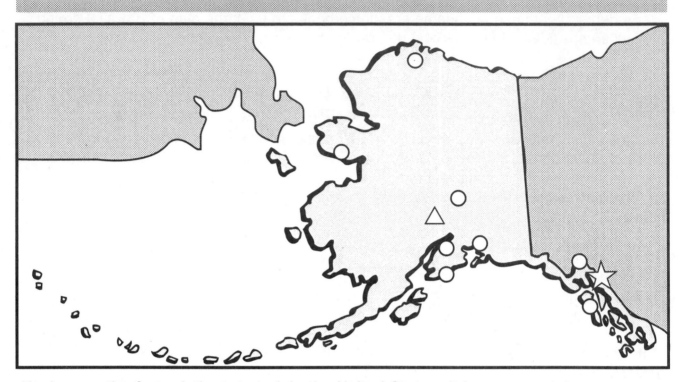

Alaska was the forty-ninth state to join the United States. It became a state on January 3, 1959. Alaska has a population of 599,151 which ranks forty-eighth among the 50 states. It has an area of 586,878 square miles (1,522,596 square kilometers), which makes it the largest state. The Alaska coastline stretches for 6,640 miles (10,686 kilometers), which is longer than all the other states' coastlines combined.

Alaska forms a large peninsula connected to North America on the east by its border with Canada. A *peninsula* is an area of land almost surrounded by water. The Bering Strait separates it from Russia on the west by only 51 miles (82 kilometers). The Arctic Ocean forms the northern boundary and the Pacific Ocean forms the Southern. Almost a third of Alaska is north of the Arctic Circle.

Alaska was purchased from Russia in 1867 by Secretary of State William Seward. He paid approximately two cents per acre (five cents per hectare). At the time, many people thought the purchase was a waste of money and labeled Alaska "Seward's Folly." However, Alaska has proven to be rich in minerals, fish, timber, and potential water power. The value of the resources taken from the state has surpassed many times the amount that was paid for the land.

The Aleutian Islands extend out from southwest Alaska off the Aleutian Peninsula and extend into the waters of the North Pacific Ocean. These volcanic islands are an extension of the Alaska Range. There are 14 large islands and 55 small ones in the Aleutians.

The Alaska Panhandle is a strip of coastal land extending 400 miles (640 kilometers) from the southeastern mainland of Alaska and along the Canadian Border. A *panhandle* is a narrow arm of land attached to a larger area. The Alaska Panhandle ranges in width from 10 to 150 miles (16 to 241 kilometers). Several mountain ranges are included in the panhandle along with the cities of Sitka, Skagway, and the capital city of Juneau.

The Alaska Mountain range is the most inland section of the Rocky Mountains. The Rocky Mountain System extends west and southwest from the Alaska-Canada Border to the Alaska Range. Among the mountains in this range is Mount McKinley, which rises to 20,320 feet (6,194 meters), making it the highest mountain in North America.

The Seward Peninsula is in the central region of the west coast of Alaska. The peninsula extends out into the Bering Strait to within 51 miles of Russia. The city of Nome is on the southern coast of the peninsula. Norton Sound forms the southern border of the peninsula and Kotzebue Sound forms the northern border.

The northern coast of Alaska is bordered by the Arctic Ocean. Point Barrow is the northernmost town in Alaska. The Brooks Mountain Range stretches across the northern part of Alaska. Prudhoe Bay, located nearly halfway between Point Barrow and the Canadian Border, is home to the largest oil reserves in North America. The Alaska Pipeline runs from Prudhoe Bay through Fairbanks to Valdez on the southern coast of Alaska.

Student Activities

Part I. Answer each of the following questions.
1. What is a panhandle? _____
2. The Alaska Mountains, which contain _____, the highest mountain in North America, are a part of the Rocky Mountain System.
3. The peninsula that extends to within 51 miles of Russia is called _____.
4. The Alaska Pipeline runs from _____ in the north to the town of _____on the southern coast.

Part II. Complete the map on the previous page by labeling each of the following places.
1. Cities or towns: Anchorage, Juneau, Sitka, Skagway, Valdez, Nome, Point Barrow, Seward, and Fairbanks.
2. Peninsulas: Alaska Peninsula, Seward Peninsula
3. Bays, inlets, and sounds: Norton Sound, Bristol Bay, Kotzebue Sound, Prudhoe Bay, Cook Inlet
4. Mountains: Aleutian Range, Alaska Range, Brooks Range, Mount McKinley
5. Draw the route of the Alaska Pipeline.
6. Bodies of water: Pacific Ocean, Gulf of Alaska, Arctic Ocean, Bering Sea
7. Straits: Bering Strait, Shelikof Strait
8. Islands: Aleutian Islands, Kodiak Island, Nunivak Island, St. Lawrence Island

Resources of Alaska

In 1890, the discovery of gold brought thousands of miners into Alaska. Towns such as Nome, Juneau, and Skagway became centers for the gold rush. Today, Alaska is still the largest gold-producing state in the United States. Much of the gold is mined from *placer deposits*. Placer deposits are particles of gold found in streambeds. Much of the gold today is found in the Yukon River near Fairbanks and near Nome on the Seward Peninsula.

Oil and natural gas are other major resources found in Alaska. The North Slope of Prudhoe Bay is home to the largest oil reserves in North America. The Trans-Alaska Pipeline was built to carry the oil southward, since the Arctic Ocean is frozen for much of the year. The pipeline runs nearly 800 miles (1,280 Kilometers) from Prudhoe Bay to Valdez on the southern shore of Alaska. The route goes over three mountain ranges and across 700 rivers and streams.

Fishing is a major industry in the state of Alaska. The Gulf of Alaska and the Bering Sea are the main fishing grounds. Salmon, halibut, cod, flounder, and herring are among the fish caught. Kodiak and Dutch Harbor are the chief fishing ports. The annual fish catch is valued at 1½ billion dollars.

Manufacturing produces about four percent of the gross state product of Alaska. Food processing, mainly fish, is the leading manufacturing activity. Salmon is processed in many coastal cities. Petroleum products rank second. There are refineries at Fairbanks, Kenai, and Prudhoe Bay. Other products manufactured in Alaska include wood products, paper products, and printed materials. The southern panhandle's coastal forest is the center of the forestry business.

The fur industry is important in Alaska. Much of this industry is found in the subarctic forest of the interior. Trappers hunt beavers, lynxes, minks, and wolves. Reindeer are raised on Nunivak Island for both food and fur. Many of the animal pelts are still used for clothing and other items for daily living.

Most of Alaska's farmland is located near Anchorage and Fairbanks. Livestock products account for approximately a third of the farm income. Milk is the most valuable livestock product, followed by eggs and beef cattle. The major crops of the state include potatoes, vegetables, and hay. Blueberries and strawberries are also harvested during the short growing season. The summer sun shines about 20 hours a day in the central part of the state, causing the crops to ripen quickly.

Student Activities

Part I. Complete the following statements.

1. The discovery of _____ in 1890 brought large numbers of miners into Alaska.

2. Define *placer deposits.* _____

_____

3. Much of the gold today is found near the two cities of _____ and

_____.

4. The largest oil reserves in North America are found at the _____ of Prudhoe Bay.

5. The Trans-Alaska Pipeline was built because _____

_____.

6. The Trans-Alaska Pipeline stretches 800 miles from _____ to

_____.

7. The leading manufacturing activity in the state of Alaska is _____.

8. Reindeer are raised on _____ Island for both meat and fur.

9. Nearly a third of the farm income in Alaska comes from _____.

10. Crops in Alaska ripen quickly because _____

_____.

Part II. Complete the following activities.

1. Make a natural resource map of the state of Alaska. Draw or trace a map of Alaska on a sheet of poster board. Develop a key of symbols to represent each resource found in Alaska. Draw the symbols on the map in the areas where the resources are found. Share your map with the class.

2. Research the gold rush of 1890. Create a map showing where the major mining centers developed. Role-play that you were one of the miners who went to Alaska searching for gold. Write a journal telling about the hardships you endured to make the journey and search for the gold. Share your journal with others in your class.

3. There was a major debate over whether buying Alaska was a good investment. In a small group, role-play that you are a member of Congress in 1867. List on chart paper as many reasons as possible why you might not have voted to purchase Alaska. Then, on another sheet of chart paper, write as many reasons as possible why you might have voted to purchase the land. Remember, the date is 1867. Decide as a group how you would have voted.

Location in Hawaii

Hawaii is located about 2,500 miles (4,000 kilometers) from Alaska in the Pacific Ocean. It is the only state in the United States not located on the continent of North America. Hawaii is the southernmost state. The island of Oahu is as far south as central Mexico.

There are eight major islands and more than 100 small ones that make up the Hawaiian Chain. The chain stretches for more than 1,523 miles (2,436 kilometers). The largest of the islands is Hawaii. Maui is the second largest. Oahu is the third in size and home to most of the population of Hawaii. Honolulu is located on the southern shore of Oahu. The other five major islands include Lanai, Molokai, Kauai, Niihau, and Kahoolawe.

Hawaii is the largest of the islands and covers 4,038 square miles (10,458 square kilometers). It is referred to as the Big Island. The island was formed by five volcanoes. Two of the volcanoes, Mauna Loa at 13,677 feet (4,169 meters) and Kilauea at 4,090 feet (1,247 meters), are still active. The Hawaii Volcanoes National Park is located in the southeast region of the island. Hilo is the largest city, chief port, and county seat of Hawaii County. It is located on the northeast coast of the island.

Maui, the second largest island, is nicknamed the Valley Island. Canyons cut into the two volcanic mountains that form the island. The highest point on the island is Haleakala at 10,023 feet (3,055 meters). Haleakala is an extinct volcano that has the largest volcanic crater in the world. The crater measures 20 miles (32 kilometers) around and reaches a depth of 3,000 feet (914 meters). The largest city on Maui is Kahului, located on the north shore just east of Wailuku, the county seat.

Oahu, the third largest island, is home to the majority of the people of the state. It is known as the Gathering Place. The island has two mountain ranges, Koolau on the eastern side and Waianae on the western side. They are separated by a fertile valley with pineapple and sugar cane plantations. Pearl Harbor, located on the southern coast, is one of the largest natural harbors in the Pacific Ocean. It has about 10 square miles (26 square kilometers) of navigable water behind a narrow entrance. Honolulu, the state capital and largest city, is located east of Pearl Harbor.

Molokai is known as the Friendly Island. The island is made up of three regions. The eastern region consists of mountains and deep canyons. The western region is dry plateau with many cattle ranches. The central region is a fertile plain where various crops grow. Molokai was the site of a leprosy colony. Father Joseph Damien was a Roman Catholic Priest who devoted his life to caring for the lepers in the colony.

Kauai is called the Garden Island because of the lush greenery and gardens. The island is circular with Kawaikini Peak at 5,170 feet (1,576 meters) in the center. Kauai also contains Mount Waialeale, one of the rainiest spots on the earth. It has an average rainfall of 460 inches (1,170 centimeters). The island also contains Waimea Canyon, which features colorful rock walls 2,857 feet (871 meters) high. It is sometimes called the Grand Canyon of Hawaii.

The other three main islands are Niihau, Lanai, and Kahoolawe. Niihau is known as the Forbidden Island, since most of the island is a cattle ranch belonging to one family. The family must give permission before anyone can go to the island. Lanai is the Pineapple Island. Ninety-eight percent of the island is owned by Castle & Cooke, Inc., the makers of Dole Pineapple. Most of the land is one large pineapple plantation. Kahoolawe is the smallest of the main islands. No one lives on the island and it is used by the U.S. Army, Navy, and Air Force for target practice.

Student Activities

Part I. Complete the following activity by writing the name of the correct island in the blank.

_____   1. the Forbidden Island.

_____   2. the Friendly Island.

_____   3. the Pineapple island.

_____   4. the Gathering Place.

_____   5. the Garden Island.

_____   6. the Valley Island.

_____   7. the Big Island.

_____   8. used by the U.S. Military for target practice.

_____   9. contains Haleakala featuring the largest volcano crater in the world.

_____   10. contains the only two active volcanoes in the Hawaiian Islands.

_____ 11. site of famous leper colony tended by Father Damien.

_____ 12. a cattle ranch owned by one family covers almost the entire island.

_____ 13. contains Mount Waialeale, one of the wettest spots in the world.

_____ 14. Pearl Harbor, one of the largest natural harbors in the Pacific, is located on this island.

_____ 15. Most of this island is a large pineapple plantation owned by Castle & Cooke, Inc.

Part II. Complete the following statements.
1. Hawaii is the only state that is not located on the _____.
2. The state of Hawaii is made up of a chain featuring _____ major islands and more than_____small ones.
3. The three largest islands of the Hawaiian Chain, from largest to smallest are _____, _____, and _____.
4. The only active volcanoes are now found on the island of _____.
5. The capital and largest city of Hawaii is _____on the island of _____.

Part III. Use the map below to label the following sites.
1. Label the eight major islands: Hawaii, Maui, Kahoolawe, Molokai, Lanai, Oahu, Kauai, Niihau.
2. Label the following cities: Honolulu, Hilo, Wailuku, Kahului.
3. Label Pearl Harbor.
4. Label the following volcanoes: Mauna Loa, Kilauea, Haleakala, Waialeale.
5. Label the following bodies of water: Pacific Ocean, Alenuihaha Channel, Kaiwi Channel, Kauai Channel

Resources of Hawaii

The tropical climate and rich *volcanic soil* of Hawaii make good growing conditions for the two major crops, pineapple and sugar cane. Every island except Kahoolawe has some type of agriculture. Most of the farmland consists of ranches or plantations owned by large companies.

Sugar cane is the most valuable crop in Hawaii. It provides about a fourth of the income from agriculture. Maui grows most of the sugar cane. Sugar cane is grown mainly on the wetter, eastern side of the islands. Pineapples are the second most important product. Again, Maui is the largest producer of pineapples.

The island of Hawaii has several large cattle ranches. Dairy and egg farms are important on Oahu. Maui and Kauai raise cattle and hogs. Hawaii exports large quantities of flowers and Hilo, on the island of Hawaii, serves as the center of the orchid-growing and flower-packaging industry.

Manufacturing accounts for four percent of the gross state product. Food processing is the leading manufacturing activity. Refined sugar and canned pineapple are the most important food products. Bread, dairy products, and soft drinks are also produced. Refined petroleum ranks as the next largest among manufactured goods. Oil from Indonesia is refined in refineries on Oahu.

Student Activities

Part I. Complete the following statements.

1. The two major agricultural products of Hawaii are _____ and

   _____.

2. The _____ and _____ provide good growing

   conditions for the two major products.

3. The island of _____ leads in the production of both pineapple and

   sugar cane.

4. The most important manufacturing activity in Hawaii is _____.

Part II. Complete the following activity.
Create a product map of the eight major islands. Design a symbol to stand for each product. Put the symbol on the islands that produce that product.

Answer Key

THE FIVE THEMES OF GEOGRAPHY

The Theme of Location   page 8

Part I

1. a. Washington, D.C.
   b. Seattle, Washington
   c. St. Louis, Missouri
   d. Dallas, Texas
   e. Chicago, Illinois

2. a. 33° 30'N, 112° 10'W
   b. 37° 47'N, 122° 30'W
   c. 35° 16'N 80° 46'W
   d. 39° 42'N. 86° 10'W
   e. 39° 45'N. 105° 0'W

Part II

3. Iowa
4. Ohio
5. Louisiana
6. Colorado River
7. Black Hills

The Theme of Place   page 9

1. geography which studies the physical and human characteristics of an area
2. physical and human characteristics
3. Both sets of characteristics are necessary to get a complete picture of a region. Each area is characterized not only by its physical setting but also by the people who live there.

The Theme of Human-Environment Interaction   page 10

1. The geography of how people change the environment and how their environment affects them.
2. There is a price to be paid when making any changes in the environment. It is important to determine whether the consequences are worth the changes that are made.

The Theme of Movement   page 11

1. people, ideas, and goods
2. The movement of people, goods, and ideas is causing each nation to become interdependent on other nations. Goods and ideas from many countries affect our lives each day.
3. When people move, they carry cultural baggage with them. They bring in new ideas about how things need to be done. The very presence of new people causes changes for others.

The Theme of Region   page 12

Part I

1. a region is an area that has a unifying characteristic that is different from the surrounding areas.
2. Regions are created to help people understand the world they live in.
3. political regions, physical regions, cultural regions, agricultural regions
4. Answers will vary.
5. Montana—Political
   Cotton Belt—Agricultural
   Great Lakes—Physical
   Chicago—Political
   Rocky Mountains—Physical
   Little Havana—Cultural
   District of Columbia—Political
   Chinatown—Cultural

NEW ENGLAND

Location in New England   page 18

1. a. Vermont
   b. Maine
   c. Rhode Island
   d. New Hampshire
   e. Massachusetts
   f. Connecticut

2. a. New Hampshire
   b. Connecticut
   c. Maine
   d. Rhode Island
   e. Massachusetts
   f. Vermont

3. a. Connecticut
   b. Lake Champlain
   c. Cape Cod
   d. Maine
   e. Connecticut
   f. Rhode Island
   g. Maine
   h. Appalachian Highlands

The Forming of New England   page 21

1. the movement and interaction of the crustal plates on the face of the earth

2. 250 million years ago
3. Himalayas; erosion and the rising of neighboring land
4. the super continent when all continental plates were joined
   The Appalachians were heavily eroded.
5. Africa; Atlantic Ocean
6. The glaciers depressed the coastal plains, and the ocean rose as the glaciers melted. The plains were covered with water.

Life in New England   page 23

1. 12; Many New Englanders work in light industry and hilly fields are not suited for mechanized farming.
2. Connecticut; tobacco, apples, fruit
3. They provided the power to allow small factories to be built along the rivers.
4. computers, machine tools, aircraft engines, and precision instruments. These industries are on the cutting edge of modern technology and should help provide for jobs well into the next century.

Inventors of New England   page 25

Inventor	Location	Date	Invention
Eli Whitney	Westborough, Massachusetts	1793	Cotton gin
Francis Cabot Lowell	Waltham, Massachusetts	1813	First American Power Loom
Elisha G. Otis	Halifax, Vermont	1852	Safe Device for Elevators
John Deere	Rutland, Vermont	1837	Steel Plow Blade
Charles Goodyear	New Haven, Connecticut	1839	Process for vulcanizing rubber
Samuel F. B. Morse	Charlestown, Massachusetts	1837	Telegraph
Cyrus Field	Stockbridge, Massachusetts	1858	Telegraph between Europe and America
Alexander Graham Bell	Boston, Massachusetts	1876	Patent for telegraph

New England States   page 27

1. 13, 228,045
2. Connecticut—25%
   Massachusetts— 45%
   Rhode Island—8%
   Maine—9%
   New Hampshire—9%
   Vermont—4%
3. 66,507 sq. miles
4. 1. Maine
   2. Vermont
   3. New Hampshire
   4. Massachusetts
   5. Connecticut
   6. Rhode Island
5. Vermont and Maine
6. New Hampshire and Massachusetts

THE MIDDLE ATLANTIC STATES

Location in the Middle Atlantic States   page 33

1. Pittsburgh
2. Baltimore
3. Washington, D.C.
4. (39° 45'N, 75° 32'W)
5. Philadelphia
6. Trenton
7. (40°41'N, 74° 12'W)
8. New York
9. (42° 35'N, 73° 47'W)
10. (43° 4'N, 76° 11'W)
11. Buffalo
12. Erie

Physical Features of the Middle Atlantic States   page 36

1. plains
2. coastal plain
3. moraine
4. Long Island
5. Piedmont
6. fall line
7. estuary
8. Finger Lakes
9. Chesapeake Bay
10. APPALACHIAN

     page 37

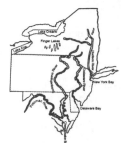

A Megalopolis
Part I
page 39

1. Boston, Massachusetts   New York City, New York
   Philadelphia, Pennsylvania   Baltimore, Maryland
   Washington, District of Columbia
2. Atlantic
3. New York City
4. Baltimore
5. New York
6. Philadelphia
7. Boston: this was the birthplace of the American Revolution
8. a region made up of two or more metropolitan areas
9. an area consisting of a central city that has a population of at least 50.000 and the suburbs that surround that city

Part II
a. Boston
b. Washington, D.C.
c. 181 years
d. 10,825,638
e. Baltimore 7%   Boston 5%
   New York City 67%   Philadelphia 15%
   Washington 6%
f. 624 sq mi.
g. 12.7%

Washington, D.C., The National Capital
Part I
page 44

1. Virginia and Maryland
2. They helped to settle the dispute over which state would be the site of the national capital. A compromise was reached that would put the capital on national territory and not in any state.
3. Dr. William Thornton
4. Philadelphia; 1800
5. Government of the United States
6. Potomac
7. Andrew Ellicott and Benjamin Banneker
8. Pierre L'Enfant
9. the rectangular blocks typical of many American cities and the wide, radiating boulevard of his native capital, Paris
10. Pennsylvania

Part II
Key to Map of Washington, D.C.

1. White House
2. Lincoln Memorial
3. Washington Monument
4. National Museum of American History
5. National Museum of Natural History
6. National Archives
7. United States Capitol
8. Supreme Court Building
9. Library of Congress
10. National Air and Space Museum
11. Smithsonian Institution Building
12. Jefferson Memorial
13. Vietnam Veterans Memorial

THE SOUTHEAST
Location in the Southeast
page 53

1. A. Frankfort, Kentucky
   B. Charleston, West Virginia
   C. Richmond, Virginia
   D. Raleigh, North Carolina
   E. Nashville, Tennessee
   F. Columbia, South Carolina
   G. Atlanta, Georgia
   H. Tallahassee, Florida
   I. Montgomery, Alabama
   J. Jackson, Mississippi
2. Charleston, West Virginia; 38° 24'N; 81° 36'W
   Mobile, Alabama; 30° 41'N; 88° 3'W
   Birmingham, Alabama; 33° 31'N; 86° 50'W
   Vicksburg, Mississippi; 32° 22'N; 90° 56'W
   Jacksonville, Florida; 30° 15'N; 81° 38'W
   Wilmington, North Carolina; 34° 14'N; 77° 54'W
3. Memphis, Tennessee; 35° 7'N; 90°W
   Louisville, Kentucky; 38° 15'N; 85° 45'W
   Huntington, West Virginia; 38° 20'N; 82° 30'W
   Savannah, Georgia; 32° 4'N; 81° 4'W
   Tupelo, Mississippi; 34° 15'N; 88° 42'W
   Greenville, South Carolina; 34° 54'N; 82° 24'W
4. a. Lake Okeechobee   e. Ohio
   b. Savannah River   f. Mt. Mitchell
   c. Tennessee   g. South Carolina
   d. Alabama

Physical Features of the Southeast
page 56

1. Atlantic Coastal Plain and Gulf Coastal Plain
2. Virginia, North Carolina, South Carolina, Georgia, and Florida
3. Florida, Alabama, and Mississippi
4. a low-lying coastal area that is often flooded by seawater
5. a swamp is a low-lying area always covered with water
6. Piedmont
7. Mt. Mitchell, North Carolina
8. Blue Ridge, Cumberland, and Great Smoky Mountains
9. Interior Plain
10. Mississippi, Ohio, Cumberland, and Tennessee
11. Dams were built to control flooding, water was provided for irrigation and power generation, conservation methods were taught, the Tennessee River has been made navigable from Knoxville, Tennessee, to where it joins the Ohio in Kentucky.

page 57

North Carolina's Outer Banks
Part I
page 59

1. sandy strips of land forming a barrier to protect the mainland
2. underwater sand bars
3. chains of rocks at or near the surface of the water
4. The Outer Banks contain shoals and reefs that have wrecked many ships.

Living in the Southeast
Part I
page 61

1. Monoculture is the growing of the same crop year after year. This practice depletes the soil nutrients. Diversified agriculture means that a wide variety of crops are now being grown in the Southeast.
2. Paper industry and furniture industry
3. Deposits of coal and iron; The local coal deposits have been mined out and imported coal must be used.
4. Fertilizer; Tampa, Florida; North Carolina; and Tennessee
5. The Piedmont region of Georgia, South Carolina, North Carolina, and Virginia
6. Lower labor costs, good port and airport facilities, less expensive land, and warm climate

Climate in the Southeast
Part I
page 63

1. The period when the temperature is always above freezing
2. hills and mountains
3. latitude and elevation
4. a tropical storm with strong winds and heavy rains
5. a climate that is damp or wet
Part II
1. Norfolk, Virginia
2. Miami, Florida
3. The temperature becomes warmer near the equator.
4. The areas near the equator receive the most direct rays of the sun.
5. the higher the elevation, the lower the temperature.

Urban Areas of the Southeast
Part I
page 65

1. Atlanta   6. Memphis
2. Nashville   7. Jacksonville
3. Memphis   8. Charlotte
4. Charlotte   9. Atlanta
5. Jacksonville   10. Nashville

Part II
1. a central city that has a population of at least 50,000 and all the surrounding suburbs
2. City Population: Jacksonville, Memphis, Nashville, Charlotte, Atlanta Metropolitan Area: Atlanta, Charlotte, Memphis, Nashville, Jacksonville

THE NORTH CENTRAL STATES
Location in the North Central States
page 74

1. Ontario, Manitoba, Saskatchewan
2. Erie, Huron, Michigan, Superior
3. Pennsylvania, West Virginia, Kentucky, Tennessee, Arkansas, Oklahoma, Colorado, Wyoming, Montana

4. Illinois, Michigan, Minnesota, Michigan, North Dakota, Ohio, Indiana, Illinois, Missouri, South Dakota, Kansas, Iowa, Wisconsin, Wisconsin, Minnesota, Nebraska, Missouri, Ohio
5. a. North Dakota   e. Kansas
   b. Wisconsin   f. Illinois
   c. Missouri   g. South Dakota
   d. Ohio   h. Wisconsin

Physical Features of the North Central States   page 76
Part I
1. plains
2. The glaciers left the northern region with scoured rocks, thin soil, and thousands of lakes. The southern region has thick, rich soils that were deposited by the glaciers.
3. Badlands are regions of small, steep hills and deep gullies formed primarily by water erosion. The Badlands are found in North and South Dakota and Nebraska.
4. Pressure from below raised the crust of the earth into a huge dome. Erosion wore this dome into the granite mountains that are called the Black Hills.
5. Ozark Plateau
6. forested hills, low mountains, many caves, large springs and lakes, and clear, fast-flowing streams
7. the Upper Mississippi River System
8. Missouri, Illinois, and Ohio

                                page 77

Chicago   page 80
Part I
1. Downtown Chicago, North Side, West Side, South Side
2. The flow of the Chicago River was changed to prevent sewage from flowing into Lake Michigan. This change represents humans changing the environment, in this case to help it.
3. The Magnificent Mile is the area around Michigan Avenue in Downtown Chicago that has many elegant stores, hotels, restaurants, and office buildings.
4. Many historians say that the fire started in Mrs. Patrick O'Leary's barn when a cow kicked over a lantern. The fire burned for nearly 24 hours. About 300 people were killed and 90,000 were left homeless.
5. Early growth factors included the location at the southern end of Lake Michigan and serving as a terminal for major railroads.
6. World's Columbian Exposition in 1893; Century of Progress Exposition in 1933.

Part II
1. a. 3,476,807
   b. Aurora-3; Evanston-2; Chicago-80; Elgin-2; Cicero-2; Joliet-2.

The Great Lakes   page 82
Part I
1. Ontario, Huron, Erie, Michigan, Superior
2. Michigan
3. 18 percent
4. As huge glaciers moved into the Great Lakes region, they pushed out deep depressions and pushed large piles of soil and rock ahead of them. As they melted, the piles of rock and soil blocked natural drainage. Gradually, over the years, the depressions filled with water, becoming the Great Lakes.
5. A series of locks and canals have been built by the governments of the United States and Canada.
6. Saint Lawrence Seaway
7. The Welland Ship Canal, located to the west of the Niagara River, allows ships to sail around the Niagara Falls.
8. The Soo Canals were built to allow ships to sail on the St. Marys River between Lake Huron and Lake Erie.
9. Ontario, Ohio, Indiana, and Pennsylvania
10. wheat, grain, iron ore, minerals, coal, copper, flour, and manufactured goods, such as automobiles and steel

Part II   page 83
1. Erie, Pennsylvania; Rochester, New York; Buffalo, New York; Gary, Indiana; Cleveland, Ohio; Windsor, Ontario; Detroit, Michigan; Chicago, Illinois; Toronto, Ontario; Duluth, Minnesota; Hamilton, Ontario; Oshawa, Ontario; Milwaukee, Wisconsin; Sault Ste. Marie, Ontario; Thunder Bay, Ontario

Agricultural Regions of the North Central States   page 85
Part I
1. Corn Belt, Wheat Belt, Dairy Belt
2. A different crop is planted in the fields in some years, so the minerals in the soil will be replenished.
3. Wheat. It is used as a food, and most people eat wheat of some kind each day.
4. Spring wheat is planted in the spring and harvested in the summer. Winter wheat is sown in the fall, lies dormant in the winter, begins to grow again in the spring, and is harvested in the early summer.
5. Wisconsin. It leads the nation in the production of cheese, milk, and butter.
6. Much of the land is used for pasture and for raising crops such as hay, oats, and corn to feed the cattle.

THE SOUTH CENTRAL STATES
Location in the South Central States   page 92
1. Mississippi, Tennessee, Missouri, Kansas, Colorado, New Mexico
2. Mexico
3. a. Gulf of Mexico
   b. Rio Grande
   c. Red River
   d. Mississippi River
4. a. Arkansas
   b. Oklahoma
   c. Louisiana
   d. Texas
5. a. El Paso   g. Amarillo
   b. Houston   h. Oklahoma City
   c. New Orleans   i. Austin
   d. Tulsa   j. San Antonio
   e. Dallas and Fort Worth   k. Baton Rouge
   f. Little Rock

Physical Features of the South Central States   page 96
Part I
1. Gulf Coastal Plain
2. Most rivers empty into a larger body of water, such as an ocean or gulf. As a river flows, the water carries small particles of soil and rock called silt. As the river nears its mouth, the flow of the water slows and the particles of silt go to the bottom of the river. Eventually, these particles build up and form new land.
3. ¼ or 25%
4. A bayou is a slow-moving inlet or outlet for lakes and rivers that serves as a natural drain for overflow water on the Mississippi River.
5. People have tried to control the flooding of the Mississippi by building levees along the banks.
6. Ozark Plateau, Ouachita Mountains, Guadalupe Mountains
7. Great Plains
8. Red, Arkansas, Rio Grande, Mississippi
9. Pontchartrain

Part II

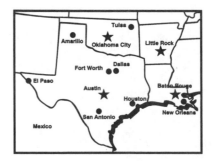

Agriculture in the South Central States   page 98
Part I
1. climate and soil types
2. Tall grassy plants that look similar to the corn plant; it is used to make syrup, feed for livestock, and in the manufacturing of brooms and brushes.
3. The South Central States produce large numbers of beef cattle that need feeding.
4. Cattle are sent to feedlots to be fed special diets that add weight before going to markets.
5. Winter wheat is planted in the fall and the roots become very strong. These roots help to keep the soil in place and guard against erosion.
6. Pests, such as the boll weevil, foreign competition; expensive mechanization; and synthetic fibers.
7. sugarcane

Urban Areas of the South Central States   page 100
Part I
1. Houston
2. New Orleans
3. Fort Worth
4. San Antonio
5. Dallas
6. New Orleans
7. Houston
8. Fort Worth
9. San Antonio
10. Dallas

Part II

City	Date Founded	Date Incorporated	Area	Major Industries
Houston	1836	1837	556 sq. miles	oil refineries, chemicals, oil equipment
Dallas	1841	1871	378 sq. miles	electronics, banking, insurance, fashion
Forth Worth	1849	1873	251 sq. miles	petroleum, grain, aerospace, cattle,
San Antonio	1718	1837	328 sq. miles	electronics, aircraft parts, food, fertilizer, clothing
New Orleans	1718	1805	364 sq. miles	petroleum chemicals metal

The Oklahoma Land Run   page 103
Part I
1. Cherokee, Chicksaw, Choctaw, Creek, Seminole
2. Many of the tribes had fought for the South during the Civil War.
3. The free land that surrounded the Indian Territory ran out.
4. May 1890; George W. Steele
5. The Oklahoma Territory and the Indian Territory

THE ROCKY MOUNTAIN STATES
Location in the Rocky Mountain States   page 112
1. a. Oregon
   b. Washington
   c. California
   d. North Dakota
   e. South Dakota
   f. Nebraska
   g. Kansas
   h. Oklahoma
   i. Texas
2. Mexico
3. a. British Columbia
   b. Alberta
   c. Saskatchewan
4. a. Idaho
   b. Colorado
   c. Utah
   d. Arizona
   e. Montana
   f. Nevada
   g. Wyoming
   h. New Mexico
                                      page 113
5. a. Santa Fe
   b. Helena
   c. Carson City
   d. Salt Lake City
   e. Albuquerque
   f. Phoenix
   g. Denver
   h. Cheyenne
   i. Casper
   j. Boulder
   k. Tucson
   l. Las Vegas
   m. Boise
6. a. Fort Peck Lake
   b. Great Salt Lake

Physical Features of the Rocky Mountain States   page 115
Part I
1. Great Plains, Rocky Mountains, Intermountain Region
2. Chinook
3. Continental Divide
4. Point at which trees do not grow
5. Great Basin, Colorado Plateau, Columbia Plateau

Part II

Agriculture in the Rocky Mountain States   page 118
Part I
1. water
2. grazing/growing wheat
3. Ogallala Aquifer
4. Missouri, Pecos, Yellowstone, Arkansas, Platte
5. Colorado Piedmont
6. cotton and vegetables
7. potatoes
8. Colorado, Phoenix, Tucson
9. Rio Grande
10. sugar beets and wheat

Urban Areas of the Rocky Mountain States   page 121
Part I
1. Phoenix
2. Brigham Young
3. Hohokim
4. Denver
5. Phoenix
6. Mormon
7. Denver
8. Central Arizona Project
9. Phoenix
10. Salt Lake City

Native Americans in the Rocky Mountain States   page 123
Part I
1. Apache
2. Utes
3. Hopi
4. Navajo
5. Navajo
6. Hopi
7. Utes
8. Jicarilla Apache
9. Hopi
10. Navajo

THE PACIFIC STATES
Location in the Pacific States   page 130
1. a. Arizona
   b. Nevada
   c. Idaho
2. Mexico
3. Canada
4. a. Salem
   b. San Francisco
   c. Sacramento
   d. Olympia
   e. Spokane
   f. San Diego
   g. Seattle
   h. Los Angeles
   i. Tacoma
   j. Portland

5. a. California
   b. Washington
   c. Oregon

Physical Features of the Pacific States
page 133
Part I
1. Coast Ranges, Sierra Nevada Range, Cascade Range
2. Mount Whitney
3. Crater Lake
4. Death Valley
5. fault
6. San Andreas
7. Willamette Valley, Puget Sound Lowlands, Central Valley

Part II

Urban Areas of the Pacific States
page 137
Part I

1. Los Angeles
2. San Francisco
3. Portland
4. Seattle
5. San Diego
6. Portland
7. Los Angeles
8. San Francisco
9. San Diego
10. Seattle

Part II
Possible Answers:

City	Date Founded	Area	Major Industries
Los Angeles	1781	466 sq. mi.	aircraft and space, movies
San Francisco	1776	129 sq. mi.	clothing, food processing
San Diego	1769	360 sq. mi.	naval & aerospace center
Portland	1845	112 sq. mi.	computer & electronics
Seattle	1852	86 sq. mi.	lumber, aircraft, spacecraft

The Oregon Trail
page 139
Part I

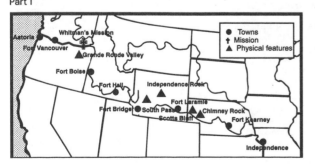

Date	Events
1805	Lewis and Clark traveled on part of the trail.
1830s	Benjamin Bonneville took first wagons over trail.
1841	Settlers began using the trail.
1842	John C. Frémont surveyed part of the Oregon Trail.
1843	The "Great Migration" took place, when over 900 used the trail.
1846	Northern boundary of territory was set.
1848	Territory of Oregon created.

Part II
1. 12,000
2. Disease, harsh climate, trees, and rocks had to be moved, danger of attack from Native Americans; danger of being washed away crossing rivers

ALASKA AND HAWAII
Location in Alaska
page 145
Part I
1. A panhandle is a narrow strip of land attached to a larger area.
2. Mount McKinley
3. Seward Peninsula
4. Prudhoe Bay; Valdez

Part II

Resources of Alaska
page 147
Part I
1. gold
2. Placer deposits of gold are found in a streambed.
3. Fairbanks and Nome
4. northern slope
5. The Arctic Ocean is often frozen and prohibits the transporting of oil from Prudhoe Bay.
6. Prudhoe Bay to Valdez
7. food processing
8. Nunivak
9. livestock products
10. The summer sun shines 20 hours a day.

Location in Hawaii
page 149
Part I
1. Niihau
2. Molokai
3. Lanai
4. Oahu
5. Kauai
6. Maui
7. Hawaii
8. Kahoolawe
9. Maui
10. Hawaii
11. Molokai
12. Hiihau
13. Kauai
14. Oahu
15. Lanai

Part II
1. continent of North America
2. eight; 100
3. Hawaii, Maui, Oahu
4. Hawaii
5. Honolulu, Oahu

Part III

Resources of Hawaii
page 151
Part I
1. pineapples and sugar cane
2. tropical climate and volcanic soil
3. Maui
4. food processing